Wo

Journeys in Prayer

101 True Stories from Many Nations

Wentworth Pike

PO Box 1047
129 Mobilization Dr.
Waynesboro, GA 30830, U.S.A.
Tel: (706) 554-1594
E-mail: gabriel@omlit.om.org
www.gabriel-resources.com

ISBN: 1-884543-66-9

Cover design: Paul Lewis

Printed in Colombia
Impreso en Colombia

Dedication

I gratefully dedicate this selection of prayer stories to my grandchildren:

Lori and Jay
Tony, Jennifer and Ruthann
Joel, JoAnne and Jeffrey
Robby and Lena

Your grandma and I have always prayed that you would each grow up in a godly, prayerful home. We continue praying that the glory of God may be manifested in each of your lives as you continue to learn the secret of the secret place. The heritage we desire to leave you is the personal knowledge of intimate, effective prayer. You cannot start too young in the school of prayer—the school from which you will never graduate.

Wentworth Pike

Contents

Foreword

Seeing God respond supernaturally to prayer is one of the most thrilling aspects of faith. It builds our spirits in ways that the best teaching, as important as it is, can never accomplish. Seeing God in action moves faith from the cerebral to the heart and spurs us on to know God better.

These stories of answered prayers and lessons the Lord teaches us through prayer, compiled by Wentworth Pike, will challenge each of us to depend on God in new ways and cause our business-as-usual prayers to be ones of expectancy and anticipation.

The Greek form of the word *faith* suggests far more than mental assent to doctrine. Biblical faith suggests *leaning*. Faith should cause us to lean continually on Jesus and His Word in such a manner that if He doesn't come through, we and our aspirations will fail. And, if our life is an "obedience of faith," we find that He always comes through. Abraham discovered that reality as expressed in Romans 4:21: Abraham was "fully persuaded that God had the power to do what he had promised."

God delights to bring us, His adopted children, into life situations where He can demonstrate how reliable it is to lean on Him. The Amplified Bible defines faith as "leaning our entire personality upon Him." The stories Wentworth has collected will revitalize you and your family, encouraging you to live experientially in faith and to enjoy going out on His limbs in faith.

J. B. Philip's translation of 1 Peter 5:7 reads: "You can throw the whole weight of your anxieties upon Him, for you are His personal concern." Living our lives in tandem with Jesus, being yoked to Him, setting anxiety aside and acting in faith all open the door of opportunities to watch Him at work. Enjoy the examples in this book of God's intervention in other's lives, and wait expectantly to see Him at work in your life and your family's.

By Jim Raymo
U.S. Director of WEC International and
author of *Marching To A Different Drummer*[1]

---

[1]Jim Raymo, *Marching to A Different Drummer* (Fort Washington: Christian Literature Crusade, 1996).

Introduction

Prayer is amazing! When Jesus taught His followers about prayer, He used stories with one and two syllable words so that even the young could understand. No method of teaching has surpassed our Lord Jesus' use of storytelling. His parables, stories from life, are so profound that they allow mystery to remain for even the most mature Christian. True stories about prayer are like that too. They can be useful tools for teaching us about the mysterious and wonderful ways of God. Samuel Chadwick said, "[God] laid down the laws of prayer, though He never sought to explain its mystery."[2] Reading about the prayer experiences of others can strengthen our family and personal devotions and encourage us to learn to pray more effectively. Blessed is the family nurtured in prayer.

As you read these stories in family devotions, you can help the children to memorize Matthew 7:7 with the following acrostic:

> **A**—"**A**sk and it will be given to you;
> **S**—"**S**eek, and you will find;
> **K**—"**K**nock, and the door will be opened to you."
> (Matthew 7:7)

Many missionaries first realize God's direction for their lives while reading missionary biographies during their early years. The missionaries' stories about answers to prayer and struggles in prayer instill strong character traits and promote spiritual growth. My hobby of collecting their prayer stories began more than thirty-five years ago. In fact, I enjoy it more than collecting stamps, sports cards or any other hobby.

When other Christians heard about my hobby, they shared their stories too. This book is a carefully balanced selection of prayer stories from various walks of life—Bible conference speakers and children, government officials and stay-at-home moms, farmers and businesspersons, craftsmen and professionals, students and teachers. There are homey stories, funny stories, cute stories, astounding miracles and practical lessons.

Answers are not the only values to be gained from prayer. Hard lessons are equally as important to all ages. Reading and hearing others' prayer experiences make Bible teaching a current, living reality, and the stories serve as trustworthy examples for making prayer our way of life. Through miracles and disappointments, the whole family learns God's valuable lessons.

A diamond's beauty is the power of its facets to reflect the brilliance of the sun; the value of these stories is their power to reflect God's glory.

Children and adults have enjoyed listening to many of

these stories in prayer seminars from Manitoba to Mexico, from Prince Edward Island to California, and from British Columbia to Florida—as well as in Asia, Africa, Europe and South America.

For your convenience, I separated the stories into different categories, but the categories do overlap. Often you'll find that a story is about Provision *and* Protection or both Guidance *and* Outreach to the Lost.

Read and discuss these stories in family devotions and reading times. Look up the places, people, climates and customs in a world atlas or encyclopedia. Check unfamiliar terms in a dictionary. As you read them, ask your family questions such as, "Billy, what does this story teach that ten-year-old boys in your school need to know?" (Avoid, "What have *you* learned?" A ten-year-old boy can discuss what *his peers* need to know without feeling that he's being singled out!) Share how the story helps you also.

And finally, please send me your stories of prayer experiences for my collection. Perhaps one will be used in a future book.

Yours in the blessed fellowship of Calvary love,

Wentworth Pike

---

[2] Samuel Chadwick, *God Listens to the Crying Heart in the Secret Place* (West Chester: Good News Publishers, 1973), p. 5.

PART ONE

Prayer Journeys of Many Folks in Many Nations

SECTION A

Suffering, Health and Healing

1

I Treated, But God Healed

Africa and North America

The brilliant North American surgeon and specialist in pancreatitis had absolute confidence in his own ability and in the successful outcome of the operation he was about to perform. In fact, he was writing an article for a medical journal outlining his procedures and near-perfect record of success with this type of surgery.

Hedley Waldock, SIM missionary to Ethiopia, had been suffering from frequent attacks of severe abdominal pain. Although the mission doctor suspected it was pancreatitis, he had been unable to make a firm diagnosis. When Hedley arrived home on furlough and had another attack, he went immediately to a clinic as the doctor had ordered. There the positive diagnosis confirmed the mission doctor's suspicions, and Hedley was sent directly to a hospital for surgery. He expected to stay a week or ten days.

The operation proceeded without any problems. However, within a short time, a fever developed, and he was unable to tolerate any food or liquid. Three weeks passed before he was permitted to go home. Even then the fever persisted, and there was some intolerance to food.

A few days after his dismissal, the trouble began all over again, and Hedley had to return for further surgery. This time the pancreas was abscessed. Again Hedley ran a fever and was unable to tolerate food and liquids.

Another two and a half weeks passed. One evening the surgeon came and sat on the edge of Hedley's bed to talk to the missionary and his wife. The surgeon admitted that he had scrapped the article for the medical journal because this case had spoiled many of his arguments. The doctor confessed to being baffled. It seemed he had come to the end of himself. All optimism and confidence were gone. He had nothing more to suggest, nothing to offer. He admitted to defeat and helplessness.

Christian friends in the United States, Canada and Ethiopia were praying.

Soon after the surgeon admitted defeat, Hedley started to improve. On a beautiful Easter morning, he was released from hospital. When he went in for a checkup, the doctor told him of an old French surgeon who used to write at the bottom of every patient's chart, "I treated, but God healed." With a degree of humility not evident before, the clever surgeon added, "This is what I have written at the bottom of your chart."

2

A Millennial Warrior's Battle

California

It was August of 1999, and the diagnosis was a declaration of war: Lymphoma cancer and leukemia complications versus fifteen-year-old Daniel Parrish. Only days before the doctor thought the pea-sized growth on Daniel's neck was an inflamed lymph gland. Its sudden growth to the size of a lemon alerted the doctors to X-ray it, and they discovered lymphoma cancer. According to Ralph Mahoney, Daniel's grandfather and Editor of *World MAP Digest,* it was "lying over his chest about seven inches wide from his neck to his abdomen."[3] This story is a condensation of the article written by Mahoney.

Grueling chemotherapy seemed to stop the growth within a few months. But in March 2000, cancer was rediscovered. Daniel's parents Frank and Wendy Parish started to send updates to prayer partners by e-mail. The following are excerpts from some of those e-mail messages.

3/3/00—Daniel's spinal tap went well. . . . three types of chemo today . . . quite sick Saturday through Monday. . . . His hair is falling out again. . . . Thank the Lord for your continued prayers and encouragement. "For the Lord our God is mighty; our help is in the Name of the Lord!"

3/9/00—This has been a difficult week for Daniel. For no apparent reason, his back, neck and right shoulder began to seize up . . . large knots in the muscles . . . severe pain . . . unable to sleep or eat . . . vomited from pain.

3/9/00—Bad news. More extensive tests showed unusual activity in white blood cells. . . . An unscheduled bone marrow aspiration revealed that the leukemia has again begun growing in the bone marrow. . . . extremely intensive chemotherapy regimen suggested . . . Our entire family feels like we have just been kicked in the stomach. . . . It seems more than he (or we) can bear to even think about, given all he's already endured. "Through the Lord's mercies we are not consumed, because His compassions fail not, they are new every morning; great is Your faithfulness. 'The Lord is my portion,' says my soul, 'therefore I hope in Him!' " (Lamentations 3:22-24).

3/11/00—Daniel was still unable to keep anything down . . . . The lymphoma is growing back as well as the leukemia. It is pressing into his trachea and perhaps even into his stomach. . . . We need God to supernaturally intervene on his behalf. We are again reminded that Daniel's life is truly in God's hands. He is the only one Who can completely heal him, and we are confident that He is able to do it!

3/15/00—The roller coaster ride continues. Current chemotherapy (is) not containing the relapse and re-growth of the cancer . . . . If there is not a definite downward turn by Friday, he . . . will be given four days of five different chemicals. It is *very* strong chemotherapy induction, intended to completely suppress the re-growth of the cancer; but it does the same to [suppresses] his immune system. This very astute young man [Daniel] who knows every detail of his treatment and keeps the entire staff on their toes with his pointed questions . . . has never doubted he would make it through this, and has been completely courageous and optimistic. However, today he said to Wendy, "Mom, for the first time since this all started, I'm getting scared." . . . And yet, where the strength of man ends is where the Almighty begins, "For in our weakness, His strength is perfected."

The March 22 e-mail from Wendy and Frank mentioned fever, uncontrollable diarrhea, vomiting, inability to eat, stomach and esophagus burning, and fluid on one lung. Although the next day Daniel's parents were somewhat encouraged because he had had a better night, and the vomiting had ceased. Unfortunately the diarrhea would not stop.

His mother Wendy stroked Daniel's head and sang:

> "Hold me close, let Your love surround me
> Bring me near, draw me to Your side
> And as I wait, I will rise up like the eagle
> And I will soar with You, Your Spirit leads me on
> In the power of Your love."

Daniel, in a weak voice, began to sing along, and they wept as they sang it over and over. Daniel said, "Mom, I want to feel the love of God surround me. I want to soar with Him." So we prayed, and asked Him to do just that for Daniel.

Amazingly, Daniel never questioned God's love, but like many of us, he wanted to be lifted to a higher place in the knowledge of the fullness of that love.

And so Daniel's unimaginable suffering continued through the end of March and on through April of 2000. His parents' e-mails contained many statements such as the following: "This week has probably been worse than the previous six months combined. . . . We have never understood to this degree the gut-wrenching pain of suffering, especially when it involves watching one of your own children. There are no easy answers. You have Job's "friends," who are sure you brought this on yourself. You have the Word, full of promises about the heritage of the righteous, yet they are seemingly unfulfilled."

4/4/00—"Daniel has absolutely stunned us with the grace of God that is being worked in and through his life. He took a small sip of diluted apple juice and was amazed that it went down, didn't hurt and stayed down. His immediate response: 'Thank you, Father. You are glorious . . . so merciful.' We were convicted to the point of tears by Daniel's tenderness. He is absolutely without guile."

On April 8, Frank and Wendy's e-mail listed ten reasons to praise God. They expected Daniel's release from intensive care soon and requested prayer for a full cancer-free recovery. Daniel said, "Dad, if I don't make it, what is the point of my life? Why would I only have sixteen years?"

Ralph Mahoney describes the scene that followed: "After a few gulps, and a moment's thought, the Holy Spirit filled Frank's mouth as he reminded Daniel that this life is really about one thing. He has had that chance to live, and to come to know the Reason he was created. He has accepted the sacrifice of Jesus, God's Son, whose blood provided the covering for sin, imperfection and weakness, in order that he might even approach this awesome and holy God. The Bible says, 'By Him and for Him all things were created.' God has made us for Himself, and once we know Him, the reason we exist is fulfilled.

"Many people try to give this life a nice face, and make it into something significant from a human perspective. But the only thing lasting is the decision one has made to believe in God and accept the sacrifice of His Son Jesus who provided a way for us to come to God. This life is just a 'bleep' on the screen of eternity. When you step back and get a 'big picture perspective', you realize how small and insignificant this temporal life really is in the grand scale of things.

"The most important thing is to keep the main thing the **main thing**. It is all about Him. Knowing Him, loving Him, serving Him, enjoying Him, worshipping Him, following Him and trusting Him. Daniel continues in God's hands. He is ultimately not our son; he belongs to God Who loaned him to us for a while to raise him to know God. Holy Spirit, lead us in these days, lead our intercession, that we might hear Your voice and know your desire."

On into May, Daniel's grueling suffering—and his family's—continued. One day, as Wendy prayed, she saw the most incredible vision of Daniel. He was tanned, muscular, and wearing armor, almost like that of Roman times but far more intricate and beautiful, as if made of silver and gold. Holding his helmet under his arm, with a broad smile, he looked at his mother "with incredible contentment, peace, joy, confidence and fulfillment . . . no pain, no anxiety, no uncertainty. It was as if he had realized everything he wanted to be; had become everything he was created for. And the Lord spoke to her and said, 'Daniel is a warrior.'"

On May 7, 2000 at 12:13 a.m., Frank and Wendy wrote,

> Dear Beloved and Precious Saints,
>
> 'Therefore… let us run with endurance the race that is set before us, looking unto Jesus, the author and finisher of our faith' (Hebrews 12:1).

Today at 3:03 p.m., Daniel finished his race as he went home to be with the Lord. It was a beautiful time that could only have been orchestrated by the Lord.

'Praise, especially when from a purely human viewpoint there is every reason for doubt and despair, is faith in full bloom' (Huegel).

'My grace is sufficient for you, for my power is made perfect in weakness' (2 Corinthians 12:9). In God's will, James' death and Peter's deliverance both glorified Him. (See Acts 12.)

[3]Ralph Mahoney, "AMillennial Warrior's Battle," *World MAP Digest,* (Burbank: World Missionary Assistance Plan, volume 40, July/August/Sept 2000, number 3). Used by permission.

3

Job's Sympathizer

Thailand

One November, missionary nurse Ruth Charter developed the first of a series of painful boils. She had been in Thailand with the Overseas Missionary Fellowship (OMF) less than two years and had just started nursing at the Saiburi Christian Hospital. When Ruth had to be off work, she prayed generally that the boils would clear up quickly because it inconvenienced others who had to fill in for her at work. But more boils came. She appreciated the specific prayers of her friends for her healing. She then asked prayer partners at home to pray. When more boils followed, she became disappointed, resentful and even angry.

Then Ruth began to realize that God was teaching her many things through this illness that could not be learned except by experience. And He had more yet to teach her. He brought her to a place of acceptance of her "thorn in the flesh" (2 Corinthians 12:7-10). He poured out His gifts: joy, faith, trust, patience, praise, rest, composure, quietness, peace, contentment and a keen sense of anticipation of the many other things He had in store for her.

But the boils persisted. Three mission doctors and a Thai skin specialist examined her and gave her prescriptions. The infection seemed to be resistant to antibiotics. People from home sent suggestions. Finally at the end of August, when there was still no physical relief, two missionary friends suggested that she write again to her prayer partners at home asking for concentrated prayer. They felt that the boils could threaten her missionary career. She accepted their counsel, and many at home prayed. One group wrote that they were covenanting that each would pray daily for her healing until the answer came.

By October 1, eleven months after they began, the boils that had plagued Ruth were completely gone, and they have never returned. She believes that the healing was from God in direct answer to the prayers of His people. Ruth will soon reach the age of retirement, but her life and career have been so different than they would have been if God had not healed her.

4

Lassa Fever!

Nigeria

In the late 1960's, media worldwide carried stories about a mysterious African disease that yielded to no antibiotics or known antibodies and killed its victims within ten to twelve hours. With jet speed, it cast a shadow of possible epidemics over two continents, Africa and North America. Sudan Interior Mission's (now SIM Int.) Evangel Hospital in Jos, Nigeria, soon found its all-out effort to isolate and conquer the virus to be hopelessly inadequate. Major U.S. health institutions almost immediately joined the battle: Yale University Laboratory in New York City, the Public Health Service and the Center for Disease Control in Atlanta.

Known to be extremely contagious, the source and method of transmission of Lassa Fever defied medical sleuths in both the field and the lab. Rats? Bats? Dust? Where did it originate, and how did it travel? There were no answers in 1969.

Nurse "Penny" Pinneo, at Evangel Hospital in Jos contracted Lassa Fever. Her racking back pains, aching muscles, ulcerated throat, swollen neck and a fever that spiked to 107 degrees left little room for hope as she was flown to a New York City hospital.

Nine years later in Miango, Nigeria, I stood meditating over the graves of two missionaries who had succumbed to Lassa Fever: Miss Charlotte Shaw and Dr. Jeannette Troup. Their graves, behind the stone chapel, were marked by simple headstones. After reflecting on their lives, I went to Jos to interviewed Penny Pinneo, a living miracle.

Question: Miss Pinneo, please bring me up to date on the Lassa Fever story.

Answer: The Lassa Fever story continues. I have just this afternoon come from our hospital where we have done a plasma pheresis on a recovered patient. Plasma pheresis is the process of taking a patient's blood, separating it, giving the red cells back to the donor and saving the serum with Lassa antibodies.

Q: Where did you get the blood for today's plasma pheresis?

A: Doctor Gwen Asten donated the blood. She has been working in a mission hospital about 200 miles north of here. Last October she became very ill, and some of the plasma that we obtained here was sent to her. She responded beautifully. She had already gone into the critical stage when her kidneys were starting to fail. Much prayer went up for her. A friend living nearby said that she had never experienced such continuous prayer as she did when she prayed for her friend Gwen. The Lord answered. She recovered, and now she is able to help others to recover from Lassa Fever.

Q: What are some other areas in which you feel prayer has been answered in regard to Lassa Fever?

A: Ever since my recovery, Philippians 1:20 has meant so much to me. It says, "Christ shall be magnified in my body, whether it be by life or by death." This was made real to me shortly after I recovered. A photographer came to my house to take my picture. He thought it would be a good idea for me to hold something up in the picture that had to do with my recovery. The book *By Life or By Death*, about the martyrs in Vietnam, was handy, and he suggested that I hold it. That became very significant because Dr. Jeannette Troup, with whom I had worked for many years, died of Lassa Fever right at the very time when the picture was taken. Her life magnified the Lord; and her death magnified the Lord. My prayer was that Christ might be magnified in me. He gave me life, and now I'm so glad to be able to continue to help others recover.

Q: How are you helping personally?

A: In giving plasma, in nursing patients and in praying for these patients who have Lassa Fever. Each year we help a number in our own hospital and in other areas of Nigeria to recover.

Q: When some have died and some have lived, why do you consider your recovery to be an answer to prayer rather than coincidence?

A: Well, the doctors said I should have died. Yet, I feel that it is the Lord who has allowed me to live.

Q: Did the virus affect some of your major organs?

A: *All* of my major organs at the same time.

Q: You mentioned glorifying the Lord whether by life or by death. Is it true that through the illnesses and deaths of Laura Wine, Charlotte Shaw, Dr. Troup and others, the Lord has enabled medical science to find some answers so that Lassa Fever is not the threat that it was nine years ago?

A: Yes. It is mainly by this plasma pheresis that we do that we have the serum.

Q: That is, you are able to use the serum from the blood of someone like yourself or Dr. Gwen Asten to inoculate Lassa Fever patients and enable them to conquer the disease in their bodies?

A: That's right. And the book, *Fever!* by John G. Fuller (Ballantine Books; New York) has been a tremendous help in telling the story. What has thrilled me so is that our testimonies are in the book, and the Lord has used that. One of our own staff members, who was ill and whose plasma was given to Dr. Jeannette, rededicated his life to the Lord after reading *Fever!* He felt that his life was not sufficiently consecrated. In the many hundreds of letters that I have received, this is the overwhelming response of people to that book: They see the need for greater dedication to the Lord!

Q: Do you mean that hundreds of people who have read *Fever!* have voluntarily written to tell you that?

A: Yes, both Christians and non-Christian readers have written. Through follow-up correspondence I have been able to develop strong friendships with them and establish a witness for Christ. And there are many individuals who tell the same story about the volume of prayer that was offered for them at the time of the illness and of the unity of the Spirit that prevailed.

Q: How long have you been a missionary in Africa?

A: Thirty-one years.

Q: Why didn't you stay at home after passing through so much suffering? Didn't you feel that you had done your part?

A: I wanted to get back to the land where the Lord had led me, the land that has become home to me and the people whom I love.

Q: What advice do you have for young people regarding missionary service?

A: Don't miss it! If that's the Lord's choice, that's the best thing for your life and you're missing His best if you don't follow through with it.

Q: But if they go into a strange land with strange fevers and viruses, aren't they liable to have to go through suffering as you have—or even have to lay down their lives?

A: Well, whatever happens, you can be enriched through it. It's worth it for what the Lord means to you in it and through it. It's a privilege to serve Him and to be willing for anything that comes. Few of us in our hospital have antibodies for patients. Sometimes I have been the only one.

Q: Then the fact that God allowed you to have Lassa Fever is part of God's answer to the prayers of many? If you had not caught it, who would provide the plasma with the necessary antibodies?

A: That's right.

Note: Penny Pinneo has retired and is living with her sister at the SIM Retirement Village in Sebring, Florida, with many of her coworkers.

5

Viper!

Nigeria

After a brief visit to her home, Laku and her friend were walking four miles to the Billiri (bil-eer-i) Bible School where they were students along with their husbands. Silently and with no warning at all, a small, deadly viper beside the trail struck Laku.

Most of the students at the Bible school were married men with families. Each family had its own small compound consisting of a mud-wall fence. They brought their grain from home and had a few chickens and a goat or two. The men had little previous education and the women even less, so courses were taught in reading, writing, arithmetic, spelling and English. Bible was taught in Hausa, a major tribal language of northern Nigeria.

Laku's friend left Laku beside the road rather than try to move her and hasten the spread of the venom. Laku's friend ran to the school and got someone to take a donkey to get her.

The mission dispensary's Nigerian staff was well experienced in treating snakebite. They seldom had any complications if they got the case reasonably soon. Laku's case appeared to be routine, so they treated her. After two days, however, Laku's condition deteriorated, so they took her nine miles to the mission hospital where a doctor was on duty.

The next day, when the principal of the Bible school and some of the teachers went to inquire about her condition, they were shocked to learn that there was little hope of recovery. The doctor declared that snakebite victims in that stage seldom survive.

On the way home, missionary-teacher Lloyd Thompson asked the Nigerian principal whether he thought they could claim the promise in Mark 16 where the Lord says if His servants should drink any deadly thing or if serpents should bite them, it will not harm them.

The principal thought for a while, and then said, "I don't see why we can't. Laku's husband Urbannus is in the Lord's service. I think that as the Lord's servants, they can claim the promise for healing."

The Bible school dismissed study hall that evening and gathered the entire student body in the chapel. Soberly, the principal told them the doctor's dire verdict and that the only hope for Laku's recovery was Lord's intervention. The students began to pray. Some asked the Lord to search their own hearts and reveal to them anything in their lives that would hinder Him from answering prayer. Many voiced definite requests for Laku's healing. The presence of the Lord seemed unusually real, and all the students felt assurance that their prayers were effective.

A few moments were taken at the end of many classes to have one or two students lead a prayer for Laku. The assurance grew that God had heard and was answering.

Slowly, Laku began to recover. The doctors and nurses were amazed. Day by day, she improved and after two or three weeks, she was dismissed. The Christian doctor and all concerned testified that her recovery was due entirely to the Lord's intervention.

It took quite awhile for Laku to regain normal strength. There was no spectacular, instantaneous healing, but everyone involved knew God had performed a miracle.

To see God work so miraculously in their midst made the Bible come alive for the students. One man said that he had studied the Bible stories and the miracles in Scripture, but he had never really related the power of God to situations today. He had looked upon the narratives of supernatural intervention as history, not as something we can expect today. To realize that God is just as much on the scene, alive and available to us today as He was to the apostles and men in the Bible was a blessing to the whole student body.

After Urbannus' graduation, he and Laku moved from their home area to start a new church, and God has blessed their ministry. Laku enjoys good health and has given birth to several healthy children since her brush with death. She is a living testimony to the mercy and power of God.

SECTION B

Guidance

6

Do You Have Any Gospels?

Iran

(This account is from an Iranian pastor who related it to Wendell Evans, the West Area Field Director of Arab World Ministries.)

"Do you have any gospels?" asked the Iranian peasant, a total stranger.

An Iranian pastor and other Iranian Christians had been driving along a road some distance from any cities, when, suddenly, their steering wheel locked. They had no choice but to stop the car. A peasant man walked up, and the pastor thought, "Maybe he can tell us where the nearest garage is," but as soon as the peasant man got to the car, he asked, "Do you have any Gospels?"

Fearing that the secret police were setting them up, the pastor answered, "What makes you think *we* would have any Gospels?"

"God told us in our village, many miles away, that if someone came to this place along this road at this hour, someone would be here with Gospels for our village. Do you have them?" asked the man.

"Yes," replied the pastor, "we do."

"Here. This is all the money we have in our village. Give me as many Gospels as this will buy."

The Christian group loaded him down with all the Gospels and New Testaments he could carry.

When they started the car, it ran perfectly. The steering wheel was no longer locked.

Many can testify today, as people did in the Bible, "As for me, the Lord has led me…." As we live daily in His written Word, He teaches us to be attuned and alert to His voice. We should not expect the kind of specific guidance to receive Testaments that the Lord gave to the Iranian peasant and his fellowship of believers, because most of us who read these words can go to a Christian bookstore and buy a Testament. But we should expect His continual guidance in His own ways for all that we need to accomplish His will.

7

Frustrating, Forgiving, Functioning

Shipboard

The large passenger accommodation on board the *Doulos*, Operation Mobilization's second ship, had a fault in the emergency lighting system, and the safety inspector was scheduled to come the next day. The emergency system lighting is extremely important in case of a blackout or fire, but for some incomprehensible reason it kept blowing out. It could take weeks to find the short circuit.

Stanley Thompson had followed his trade as professional electrical engineer for twenty-five years on the big passenger ships of the Cunard Line. When he left secular employment for full-time Christian service, he served on the *Logos* and then as program coordinator for OM. When OM purchased the *Doulos*, Stanley spent a few months sorting out the problems. There was one mystifying problem left and only one day to find and correct it.

"I tried all the tricks that I had learned over the years to locate the difficulty quickly, but I couldn't. Suddenly, while walking along one of the passageways in the passenger accommodation, I thought, 'Why haven't I taken this to the

Lord?' So I prayed, 'Lord Jesus, I ask Your forgiveness for struggling and being frustrated. Forgive me for not bringing this to You. I know that You are the Creator and the Source of all knowledge, and I acknowledge You for who You are and what You are. Now, Lord, You know where the fault is; You know what is causing this problem. Please show me where it is.'

"As soon as I finished praying, I was led to walk to the other side of the ship and down into a passageway, a place I would never have dreamt of going. I took a small ladder from a bunk in the cabins and climbed to a fluorescent light fixture. Taking down the fixture, I saw behind the fitting. Some water had run down onto the cable and was causing the short circuit. In five minutes I repaired it and we got the safety certificate."

Stanley soon learned to pray about practical matters. He was working in the engine room of the ship. While he had been on leave, a high-speed generator had been taken ashore, repaired and reinstalled. Before sailing, Stanley asked whether it had been tested. Assured that it had, he thought no more about it until, three days at sea, the generator was needed and found to be faulty.

Trying everything he knew and being unable to determine the source of the trouble, Stanley was in a state of frustration. The machine had been completely dismantled to make the repairs and no one could now find the error without going through the same procedure entirely. Instead, the highly trained engineer, now a babe in Christ, was learning the simplicity of childlike trust in his Savior. He went to his cabin, got down on his knees and prayed.

Back in the engine room a few minutes later, it was as though unseen hands had hold of Stanley's hands, guiding him to undo some nuts from bolts on straps inside the engine.

Turning over the straps, he found markings that indicated they had been crossed over.

"I would never have taken those things off to check them," he recalls. "They had been marked on the outside, but they were put back on the underside, where they could not be seen, and had been crossed over. I just changed the straps over, pressed the button and praised the Lord!"

Such experiences teach us that prayer is not limited to formal or stated prayer times, or to panic prayers, but it is a walk in fellowship with and dependence on the Lord.

8

God's Guidance in Giving

England

Letter after letter, from one Christian organization after another, included a self-addressed envelope in their correspondence. Another appeal for money. A person would like to help them all, but there is a limit. Mrs. Marguerite Peer could not prevent the negative feelings she was developing, so she sought God's guidance in the matter.

While on a visit to England for several months, Marguerite decided that her accumulating tithe money should be put into active service. She knew of three British organizations that had a policy of not asking for funds. As she prayed, she had a strong prompting to send some money to one where she would not normally be inclined to give.

Placing the money in British currency in an envelope, she felt a check in her spirit. So, she went back to prayer. She was confused. It was not really the organization she would have chosen. At last, although unable to explain her actions, she had peace about the Lord's direction. Removing the British currency, she replaced it with an American pension check she had just received that was equivalent in value.

Several days later, a letter from the Christian group told of a praise meeting held by the staff. While Marguerite was praying for guidance, they were praying urgently for the very sum she decided on. Since the currency exchange rate was very tight at that time, they asked the Lord that he provide the needed funds in American money so they could clear off an obligation to an American organization.

9

An Opera Singer Performs on Skid Row

Detroit, Michigan

Jerome Hines, world-renowned basso with the Metropolitan Opera Association, speaks of the Bible as "the libretto of [his] life," and unhesitatingly tells about accounts of God's guidance and protection in answers to prayer.

Critics for the *New York Post*, the *New York Times*, the *News Tribune* and other respected newspapers are unusually profuse in their praise of Hines' performances. He has sung for presidents and kings, and he toured the Soviet Union long before its demise. When he sang at the Bolshoi Opera, Kruschev led a standing ovation.

Harriet Johnson, writing in the *New York Post*, described him as "probably the most modest major artist before the public today," and added, "Hines is a man of big stature, 6 ft. 6 in." . . . He keeps thin by workouts at a gym, is soberly handsome and big in spirit as well as physique.

"In religion he is a man of action, a working member of the Salvation Army, who not only has sung many benefits for them, but contributed endlessly of his time and energy to help derelicts and others who are down and out."

The following story is one of Hines' experiences in prayer.

"The Voice Within"[4]

There was the occasion in Detroit early in my Christian life when God first spoke to me about working on skid row. I say first because it was the first of many such assignments He was to send me on.

After checking into my hotel room, I asked God just where He wanted me on skid row. The answer came back.

"Come with Me, and I'll show you."

Soon I was wandering through an area of bedraggled flophouses and dingy bars. "God, what in the world am I doing here?" I asked as I passed a drunk dressed in rags. I tugged self-consciously at my tie.

Then I saw a familiar sign: SALVATION ARMY.

I decided to enter, but to my astonishment, as I reached the building, the voice said, "Not here. Keep walking."

I started to argue: I knew people in the Army, I could give names to introduce myself—but I caught myself in time and kept walking.

At last, many blocks later, I came to a building on which the words RESCUE MISSION were written. And now the voice inside me unmistakably said, "Here."

So this was my job for tonight! A little embarrassed, I walked inside, introduced myself to the minister and asked if I could help out at the mission in any capacity. He looked at me oddly and the answer was a cold, "No."

After an embarrassed silence, I asked awkwardly if I could sing for their service that evening, adding hastily, "You see, I'm in town on a singing engagement . . . I sing at the Metropolitan Opera House."

He was unimpressed. "No," he said again.

I started to leave when he called after me: "Do you think you can work your way into heaven by doing good deeds?"

In answer, I simply said, "I came here because God sent me."

This statement aroused his interest and led me to tell him of the experiences that had brought me to know Jesus Christ.

By the end of my story, his attitude had totally changed. He told me that an outside church was coming to hold the evening service and that he had not wished to interfere with their program. Now he felt God really had a place for me in that service. It was quickly arranged that I should sing.

That evening I was about to leave for the mission when my accompanist, Emil Danenberg, arrived at the hotel—four hours ahead of schedule.

"Where are you off to, Jerry?" he asked.

"I've . . . ah . . . we've got a concert," I told him. "Come on."

Without a word, he followed me through shabby streets to the mission. The man leading the program greeted us with great relief.

"Thank God!" he cried. "Thank God you came!"

He almost dragged us inside. "There's been a mix-up," he said. "No one has showed up for our program tonight, and the men are getting restless." Then his face fell.

"Oh, but my wife's sick! There's no one to play the piano!"

"The Lord has taken care of that," I said, pointing to Emil.

"Can he play hymns?"

"I'll try," answered Emil—a world-famous concert pianist.

So Emil played, and we had a meeting there none of us will ever forget. Not only were there a lot of men, but they were ready, eager, and waiting with an expectancy that charged the air. Lives were changed that night and hearts opened—our own included—in such a way that left no doubt Whose meeting it was and Who had called each of us to that place.

So I know with great certainty that I have heard and continue to hear His voice— and receive His help. It comes as long as I continue to turn to Jesus, as long as I continue to ask for His guidance, and as long as I am willing to obey His instructions when I receive them.

"His sheep follow him because they know his voice" (John 10:4).

[4]Used by permission of Christian Arts Inc.; 1755 West End Avenue, New Hyde Park, Long Island, New York 11040.

10

I Am The Way

Minneapolis, Minnesota

Derek de Cambra is an associate of Jerome Hines, who wrote and performed the Christian opera "I Am the Way." (See the preceding story about Jerome Hines.) Derek is Artistic Director for Christian Arts, Inc. He kindly contributed this story for *Worldwide Journeys in Prayer.* As a first-person account, it is best told in Derek's own words.

"Neither rain, nor sleet, nor snow, nor gloom of night will stay these couriers from their appointed rounds" is the slogan that applies to letter carriers of the postal service.

This slogan may well have applied to the 4,500 ticket holders on March 27, 1975, who braved one of Minnesota's worst blizzards to attend the sacred opera, "I Am the Way," by Jerome Hines, at the Northrop Auditorium in Minneapolis. From early morning of that memorable day the weather reports held no promise of a letup of the snowstorm that began the night before. By mid-afternoon most social and religious functions scheduled for that Maundy Thursday evening were cancelled because of the hazardous traveling conditions.

As Director of the opera, I alone was faced with the

decision "to postpone or not to postpone." We had a sold-out house and were already committed to many contracts involving more than a hundred people and several thousands of dollars. Realizing that many of our soloists, the orchestra and the theater itself were not available for any other time within the next three weeks, I could not postpone. Cancellation was unthinkable, for not only would this result in a paralyzing financial loss for CAI (Christian Arts Inc.), but cancellation would make us vulnerable to many lawsuits for breach of contract. In addition to all of this, we would disappoint thousands of ticket-holders. After much prayer and consultation with key persons involved in the production, my decision became quite clear. The opera would be performed as scheduled.

The Lord blessed this decision, for not only did we have practically a full house (4,500 people out of a possible 4,700), but many who would not have come to an opera on the life of Christ came as replacements for relatives and friends who were snowbound. Many of the last-minute replacements were deeply moved, and some, judging from their responses, went away from the Northrop Auditorium that evening with changed lives because of the impact that "I Am the Way" had upon them.

The Minneapolis production of "I Am the Way" can best be summed up in the words of one of the attendees who expressed the sentiments of many others: "I thoroughly enjoyed the production. My eleven-year-old went, and he too was quite impressed. We were glad we did venture out in the bad weather to see this marvelous production. This was truly a once-in-a-lifetime experience. Thanks to all of you for this marvelous production that we shall never forget."

"Jesus answered, 'I am the way, the truth and the life. No

one comes to the Father except through me'" (John 14:6). "I will instruct you and teach you in the way you should go; I will counsel you and watch over you" (Psalm 32:8).

11

Lord, Your Name is at Stake!

Saudi Arabia

Facing a lawsuit of 10,000 rials (about $2,500) against their company, the three brothers came to the end of a busy Sunday in their lawyer's office. In the Muslim world of Saudi Arabia, Friday is the holy day; Sunday is just another business day. The oldest brother, Muthu, was a Hindu and originally from India, but he had formed a company in Saudi Arabia providing maintenance and repair of business machines and projectors. Having contracts for all such jobs with the U.S. Armed Forces in the country, he had become very successful financially and planned to guide his brothers in the business so that they could share in his success. He was irate when they converted to Christianity.

As they left the lawyer's office, Muthu gave his brother Moni, who was younger by twenty-five years, a file of important papers that needed to be returned to the company office. Muthu took the company car and the two younger men hailed a taxi to take them to the evening service at the church.

Although legally equal partners, Raja, who was the second

oldest, and Moni took orders from their brother according to the Hindu custom of their family. Usually, as church time drew near, Muthu would try to keep them too busy to go to church. Time after time, however, the Lord enabled them to complete the job in time to go. Muthu still complained that they were neglecting their work by going to church.

Instead of returning to the office with the file, they took it with them. In haste, Moni left the papers in the cab. When the loss was discovered, Moni and Raja had no means of identifying the taxi. They went to the office of the traffic police, but were told that there was no way to find the papers unless they knew the number of the cab.

Returning to their office, the Christian brothers took a company car and began searching. For twenty-four hours they drove around the city, checking all the cabs they could find.

When Muthu heard about the loss, he was furious. He raged about the Christians' God who caused them to leave their work to worship Him but who could not help when they were in trouble.

Raja and Moni were frustrated. After two days, with still no sign of the missing file, Raja, his wife Emily, and Moni prayed in desperation, "Lord, Your name is at stake. Please help us to find the file, and if You can't help us find it, then we are not going to follow You any more." Looking back on the incident, both men, now more mature Christians, realize it was a foolish prayer of babes in Christ, but God had mercy on them.

Driving to the seashore, a seldom-visited area, they spotted one taxi. "Is that the cab we rode in?" cried Moni. Stopping their car, he jumped out and ran to the cab driver.

"Do you remember me?" he asked.

"Yes," replied the driver, "and I have your papers in a safe place. I didn't know where you live, so I couldn't return them to you."

Muthu never again forbade Raja and Moni to go to church. In later years, in answer to the prayers of many, Muthu also received Jesus Christ as his personal Savior.

12

A Bible for a Russian Congregation[5]

Siberia

(The following took place in the U.S.S.R. before its collapse.)

"Go to the town at the end of the line," God seemed to be telling Jim. Exhausted from his several weeks of travel in the Soviet Union, Jim, a Christian from the West, slumped into a train seat and pressed his cheek against the steamy window. "Go to the end of the line?" he thought; "Where I'd really like to go is home!"

But Jim did not go home. Instead he took the train to the little town at the end of the tracks. After a quick supper in an old brick hotel, he wandered through the streets looking for a church.

Perhaps that was why God led him to this town. Maybe he was to encourage the believers here. But after several hours, he had found no church. Tired and baffled, he went back to the hotel and went to bed.

The next morning, before he got up, the receptionist rang his room. "Someone is here to see you," she said.

Jim dressed swiftly. He picked up a Russian New Testament from under the shirts in his suitcase and shoved it into his briefcase. "It's safer here," he reasoned as he hurried out the door with the case.

In the lobby, a middle-aged man grasped Jim's hand enthusiastically and introduced himself by name. "Can we talk in this corner?" the man asked, already leading Jim toward a chair.

"You have something for me in your case," the man said as they sat down. Jim stiffened with fear but tried to keep his face relaxed and emotionless. He knew the KGB had shadowed him during his trip. Twice, luggage left in his room had been searched. Besides, this Bible was his last copy. He had given the others to grateful Christians.

"But, I might as well give him the Bible if he asks," Jim thought. "If he is from the secret police, he will get it anyway."

"I have only my personal belongings in my briefcase," Jim hedged.

"You have a Bible for me, don't you?" the man persisted. His gray-blue eyes glistened as he looked anxiously at Jim. Resigned to the inevitable, Jim took out the Bible wrapped in tan paper and placed it in the man's hands.

The man ripped off the paper, pressed the Bible to his lips, kissed it and fell to his knees praising and thanking God in a loud and jubilant voice.

Shocked and relieved simultaneously, Jim shook the man by the shoulder, "Be quiet. We'll get in trouble. Let's go outside."

"How did you know who I was and that I had a Bible?" Jim asked.

Walking with him in the park still drizzly with sunlit streams and puddles after a morning rain, the man told Jim his story.

"Three weeks ago on a Sunday, our church—there are over ninety members—knelt in prayer asking God to provide us with a Bible. Not even our pastors had one. An elderly man in the congregation stood up in the middle of prayer and said, 'God has told me that a man named Jim will be in the town of _______ three weeks from today. He will give us a Bible.'

"So my church sent me as their messenger. That is how I knew who you were. God led me to you."

"What city did you come from?" asked Jim.

"From ___________, Siberia."

"That's a long way," gasped Jim.

"Yes, it is," said the man. "Over 6,000 miles. And it took me exactly three weeks to get here."

---

[5]Reprinted by permission from Slavic Gospel News, Box 1122, Wheaton, IL 60187.

13

Mary Poppins in Action

Zambia

(By Sandra Levinson of Alliance for Children Everywhere, an ACTION partner ministry.)[6]

"We call her Mary Poppins. Granted, most of our children in Zambia have never seen *Mary Poppins*. Nevertheless, Marie Meaney, an ACTION missionary from Seattle, Washington, is Mary Poppins to the children and to us. Marie, like Mary Poppins, brings life to children and children to life. She walks around the filthy, dusty compounds of Lusaka with pointed-toe beige shoes tied with satin bows. She always wears her trademark straw hat, so enormous that if you didn't know better, you would think it was a walking basket. Yet, everywhere Marie goes children follow her. These days she goes directly to the Resource Center. It is there you will find children.

Marie is retired with a Ph.D. in education. She arrived in Zambia in June for a short visit. Her passion and desire was to reach the poorest children with the delights of learning. For a Zambian child, living in a dark, drab, colorless world, that would be a great feat and treat. The majority of the children in Zambia (65%) are too poor to attend school. Now, we all love, admire and respect Mrs. Meaney, but the idea of a center such as this was a great stretch of faith for us, both from a practical standpoint and a financial one. Would anyone actually sponsor such an idea?

Marie returned to Zambia in August with her double-foot amputee husband, Mike, ready to change peoples' minds about children who were slow learners and those who were bright but would never get a chance to excel in their abject poverty. In faith Action International Ministries pledged the start-up funds to build the center, and in less than two weeks the building was ready. Prior to her arrival a message from Marie via e-mail said to paint the inside rooms either mauve or light honey. We all had a good laugh trying to figure out who in Zambia had ever even heard of those colors. We finally found a tablecloth with mauve in it and took it to the paint company to match.

Without jet lag or fatigue, the day of arrival found Marie on our large front lawn with ten of our Zambian friends unpacking fifteen cartons, some of which British Airways had agreed to take as extra baggage without extra cost. She had everything from colored fish to soccer balls, yards of yarn and Bible story cards, furry slippers and animals and *National Geographics* and bubbles. The Zambian team was good-natured and helpful, but none were convinced that all of this "stuff" was really going to make any difference at all in the lives of orphans, street children and the poorest of the poor.

Well, we were all very wrong! I could share story after story with you about the impact this Resource Center has already had on these children, and the official opening is still a week away. The real purpose of the center is to evaluate the child's strengths and weaknesses and develop a special set of programs for them using the tools and elements of the center. For example, on one of the first days after Marie returned, Simon, a fifteen-year-old who functions at about age seven, followed Marie to the center. She already had evaluated him and knew that he did many things at once, got frustrated, and did not finish things well. Marie showed Simon a tropical fish. He had never seen one and was delighted by the colors and shape. Asked if he would like to make one himself, he was all smiles and energy.

The next afternoon Simon found me playing with one of the babies and grabbed me away. He took my hand and led me to the Resource Center. Inside he pointed to the ceiling, and there hanging by some wire from one of the ceiling rafters was a beautiful, colorful tropical fish. Simon, proud as a peacock, said, "That's my fish. I made it yesterday." The next day Simon was an expert on tropical fish. He read about them in *National Geographic*, knew how long they lived and why they had so many colors. He also knew God made fish and on which day God made them. To Simon's way of thinking, he was closer to his Creator because of that paper and paint fish.

This afternoon around 4:00, I again stopped by the Resource Center to see if Marie was ready to quit for the day. Yes, she does get tired! There on the floor was a small dust bowl of a boy without shoes and with holes in his clothes. He was kneeling on the concrete floor very intent on something. For the first time in his life he was trying to put the pieces of a large puzzle together. When done, he looked up and asked our Mary Poppins what the animal was in the picture.

"Why, that's a rabbit," Marie said.

Our little boy asked, "What's a rabbit, Mrs. Meaney?"

You can be assured that our little boy, now curious, will be following the trail of Simon to the books and the pictures to learn more about life and about rabbits. Through his exploration his mind will be expanded, his senses alerted and his curiosity will lead him to learning. Marie calls the child's self-learning experience "*eureka*!" We call it blessed. We praise God for Marie's vision and faithful pursuit of children's minds and imaginations. Marie Meaney is not retired but re-fired, and we are grateful and honored to have her in Zambia. The hungry, drab, gray world of these poorest children has suddenly burst into glorious color for the glory of God! In the glorious color that Christ brings!

---

[6]*Zambia Resource Center—For the Mind of a Street Child and the Glory of God!* From Action International Ministries' (ACTON) Web Site: www.actionintl.org.

14

The Atheist's Prayer

Toledo, Ohio

"How do I begin to believe in God when I haven't believed all my life?" scoffed Leslie Middleton. "I am an atheist. I can't believe now!"

When Mrs. Mary Goforth Moynan, daughter of the late, well-known missionaries Jonathan and Rosalind Goforth, was asked for her favorite prayer story, she responded excitedly, "Oh, yes, one comes to mind immediately!" I thought she would tell me of her childhood in China, perhaps one of her mother's wonderful stories of God's leading or revivals from the early days. But she had some of her own.

"Looking back over my seventy-five years, I feel that this is the most rewarding type of ministry that I have had a part in. I maintained a liaison between the women's prayer groups in our churches and the minister, my husband Bob. He would give me a list of specific requests for prayer. He believed, and I do too, in very specific prayer requests. Bob would share a problem with me without mentioning the name, and I would take it to the women's prayer group."

On one occasion Pastor Bob Moynan went personally to the ladies' group at Collingwood Presbyterian Church in Toledo, Ohio, because he was very agitated in his spirit about a certain case. He told them, "This is the hardest nut I've had to crack."

A doctor in the congregation had called him with a request that he visit Mr. Leslie Middleton, who was in the hospital with terminal cancer. Middleton was an atheist. Bob made a visit, but couldn't get anywhere with him.

"I've been planning all my life for my retirement," said Middleton. "Now that I have cancer, I haven't any retirement. I haven't got a thing to look forward to."

As Bob tried to persuade him to put his trust in Christ, Leslie Middleton countered with, "How do I begin to believe in God when I haven't believed all my life?"

So Pastor Moynan asked the ladies' prayer group to pray specifically. "Please pray that I will be given the passage of Scripture that will reach this man's heart."

On the way to the hospital, it was as though a light from heaven came to him. The passage from Mark 9, concerning the boy possessed with an evil spirit, flashed into his mind.

Pastor Moynan told the Bible story to Leslie Middleton. When he read verse 24, "Lord, I believe; help thou mine unbelief," the atheist's face lit up. "Bob," he said, for by then they were on a first-name basis, "you've gone 'round and 'round with me, but this time you've hit the bull's eye. Even an atheist can pray that prayer." And he did; he prayed. "Help thou mine unbelief." From that moment, he was a saved man.

Leslie said, "Bob, everyone in this part of Ohio knows that I have been a hard-nosed businessman and an atheist all my life. They will come from all over the Toledo area to my funeral. Bob, I want you to preach at my funeral and tell everyone about my salvation. And, Bob, have them put on my tombstone, "Lord, I believe."

Leslie was right in that his reputation and mean disposition were well known. His funeral was well attended, and the story of his salvation made a profound impact.

Two years later, Pastor and Mrs. Moynan went to Brazil to organize an English speaking church. While there, they met Mr. and Mrs. Hehner. Mrs. Hehner was an avid fan of Rosalind Goforth, Mrs. Moynan's mother. She had read all the books Mrs. Goforth had written, so the Moynans and the Hehners became close friends.

Both families returned to the States. When the Moynans visited their friends in Franklin, Indiana, Nels Hehner brought out some pictures. As Bob looked at one, he exclaimed, "Why, I know that spot. I buried a man right there, and his tombstone has on it, 'Lord, I believe.'" Then he told the story of Leslie Middleton's conversion without mentioning his name.

As the story progressed to the climax, Nels burst out, "You *can't* mean Leslie Middleton!"

"Why, yes. Did you know him?"

"Know him? I worked for him for years. That man was a confirmed atheist and the hardest man to work for I've ever known! Mr. Moynan, you were led by God to tell me this story. It is the most wonderful answer to prayer that I have ever heard. Only God could change a man like Leslie Middleton."

[illegible] about my own affairs. You [illegible] have [illegible] out of my own head [illegible] I [illegible]."

[illegible] were well known and the funeral was well attended, and the [illegible] of the [illegible] made a profound impression.

[illegible] Poirot and Mrs. [illegible] went to [illegible] Church [illegible] lunch. While [illegible] Mr. and Mrs. [illegible]. Mrs. [illegible] was an [illegible] fan of [illegible] Church [illegible] Mr. [illegible] had [illegible] the [illegible] had written [illegible] and the [illegible].

[illegible] When the [illegible] brought [illegible] at the [illegible] for [illegible] son of [illegible] conversation [illegible] his name.

[illegible] and [illegible]

"[illegible] you know him?"

[illegible] man was [illegible] and the [illegible] man [illegible] I have [illegible] you were [illegible] to tell me this [illegible] that I have ever heard [illegible] like [illegible]

15

Fasting and Prayer

Northern Canada

"I believe that fasting is sometimes an integral part of effective praying," testifies Gary Crumbaugh. "Or at least it seems that there are times when it is necessary for real power. Every time that I can recall having spent several days in fasting, God has done something special."

Gary was concerned because he had not baptized any Indian converts through his ministry in Canada. After prayer and fasting, he had the privilege of baptizing two native people.

Once, after three days of prayer and fasting, Gary had a call from Stanford, a native Indian from Winnipeg. "Could you come and pray with me?" Stanford asked.

Stanford had been to the church services before, and Gary had even prayed with him from time to time. Still, Gary admitted that it didn't seem that Stanford had much potential for becoming a true believer. He had seemed hard and sarcastic and had appeared to be ridiculing the services.

Stanford was concerned because another Indian had put a curse on him, and Stanford had developed distressing stomach symptoms. He had visited the medicine man twice and a medical doctor once, but there was no relief. He thought he would die.

Gary and his wife Carol prayed with him. He got on his knees and, in the name of the Lord Jesus, renounced all forms of the occult in which he had been involved. Then he gathered all his Indian medicines, took them to Crumbaughs' home and burned them in the stove. He then was baptized.

Afterwards, Stanford faced a lot of opposition at home; his mother still held to the practice of occult Indian medicine. Stanford experienced periods of backsliding and rededication as well as many struggles and needs for prayer. Still, God used Gary's time of prayer and fasting to bring Stanford to a place of willingness to call him when he needed help.

16

A Golden Crown for the Golden Years

Quebec and Thailand

"I would like a missionary project. Is there some way in which I can become involved with someone associated with the hospital in Saiburi? I'm seventy-eight years old," wrote Marion Robertson.

Helen Bacon had received many letters from folks back home in Canada wanting to know all about Thailand, but this one was different. In all her years of missionary service in south Thailand with the Overseas Missionary Fellowship (OMF), she had never received one quite like it.

"Dear Auntie Marion," Helen's response began, for that is the way the Thai would address an elderly lady who is not a blood relative. And so it was that Miss Marion Robertson of Montreal was introduced to Doy, a young Buddhist girl under Helen's tutelage in the hospital operating room. Doy had little knowledge of Christ and was deeply involved in Buddhist practices and heathen festivals. Marion's project was clear: Pray for Doy's conversion.

A prayer partnership formed between Helen and Marion, twelve thousand miles apart, based on the promise, "I tell you that if two of you on earth agree about anything you ask for, it will be done for you by my Father in heaven" (Matthew 18:19).

About two years after Marion's original inquiry, Doy was saved. Marion's excitement about answered prayer grew, so she wrote, "What should I pray for next?"

"Not until Doy accepts baptism," wrote Helen, "will the national Christians believe that she has really put her trust in Jesus." Marion's second project: Pray for Doy's baptism.

Auntie Marion was well past eighty years old when word came that Doy had been baptized. "Well, now what do I pray for?" she queried.

In Thailand only about one-tenth of one percent of the people profess Christianity, and some of those who profess are not born-again believers like Doy. When a Christian Thai girl marries into a non-Christian home, the pressure to revert to Buddhism is usually overpowering. A major need was to find Doy a Christian husband. Project number three: Pray for a Christian husband for Doy.

Marion eagerly read the letter that told of Doy's boyfriend, but alas, he was not a Christian. She redoubled her efforts in intercession until another letter said that the boyfriend had made a profession of faith. Helen's excitement was tempered because she feared that he might have done so in order to marry Doy. Back to the firing line of prayer warfare marched the elderly woman.

The wonderful crowning point in prayer partnership came when Helen wrote that Doy's boyfriend had not only been genuinely born again, but he had also been baptized, was witnessing to his parents and friends, had led others to Christ and was active in the local church. The wedding date was set for the founding of a new Christian home, one founded upon prayer and the Word of God in south Thailand. Miss Robertson rejoiced in Montreal as the angels rejoiced in Heaven!

17

A Former Mulsim Learns About Prayer

Nigeria

Hajara was childless, a disgrace in her Hausa culture, and her Muslim husband had sent her away. She married another Muslim, but she still had no children and was divorced again. When her third husband sent her away, her parents and all her relatives mocked her and said that she wasn't worth anything because she was childless.

Hajara was very troubled, but in Kano, Nigeria, at the SIM Eye Hospital, she became a Christian. Still unschooled in the Christian faith, she married again, this time to a Christian man in Kaduna. There, she got a job working for the missionaries, George and Ruth Foxall, doing housework.

One day, Ruth was talking to some Christian friends about the importance of one-to-one discipleship. Later, she commented to George, "I wonder what I could do. Who I could work with?"

"Well, you have someone coming to our house every day," he replied. "Why don't you talk to Hajara?"

Hajara began studying a theological-education-by-extension (TEE) programmed textbook called, *Talking With*

God. She did the assignments at home every day, and once a week she and Ruth reviewed the lesson together.

One day Hajara told Ruth that God had really been speaking to her through the lessons. "I know God has the power, and He answers prayer," she said.

Both Ruth and Hajara were praying about Hajara's childless state. One day Hajara said, "I've just given it to the Lord. I know He can move mountains, but I'm satisfied. If He wants me to have a child, He will give me one. And if not, I'm satisfied." Together, they rejoiced that Hajara had so completely given herself to the Lord that He could do as He pleased.

Eventually, Hajara had a lovely daughter named Hannatu. In Hajara's village in northern Nigeria where she returned, according to the custom, to have her baby, everyone was amazed. A few years later, God gave her another daughter, Rifkatu. Truly, God answered Hajara's prayer in His own time and for His glory.

18

An Overpowering Burden

Chicago, Illinois

When Bill Pencille (pronounced "pencil"), a missionary to an unevangelized tribe in South America, looks back to his student days at Moody Bible Institute, he recalls an answer to prayer that he will never forget.

A letter came from his mother in California that said Bill's brother Norman, twelve years younger than he, was ill. "But," Bill reasoned, "Norman is just a child, and childhood diseases come and go." He may have mentioned the matter in prayer once or twice, but he did not become overly concerned about it.

On a Sunday night, around ten o'clock, Bill sat down at his desk to glance over the next day's lessons and spend a few minutes in Bible reading and meditation before retiring.

"Suddenly, an overpowering burden came upon me for my brother," recalls Bill. "I offered a brief prayer for him, but the burden didn't lift. Finally I was forced to get out of my chair, kneel and specifically lay Norman before God in prayer, even though I had no idea what the need was. I realized, of course, that he had been sick, but there had been no further word. After several minutes of prayer the burden lifted. I thanked the Lord and went to bed."

Because the mail was slow during World War II, another week passed before the next letter arrived from California. It was all about Norman, whose severe illness became progressively worse until the previous Sunday evening, when it reached a crisis.

"All of a sudden," wrote Bill's mother, "at about eight o'clock in the evening, the fever passed, and he drifted off to sleep. When he awoke, he had no sign of the illness, no symptoms whatsoever."

Eight o'clock! Two time zones east of California, it had been ten o'clock—the precise time when Bill had been on his knees praying in Chicago.

19

Who Are You to Judge?

Japan

The tension was mounting. Dan, supervisor of the Japanese language school for new missionaries, could not get one man to cooperate. Outwardly, the stubborn student smiled and appeared very pleasant. But beneath the façade was an obstinate disposition. Dan was in charge of the schedule for the language courses. He assigned one name to this teacher, another to that one. When he came to the name of the headstrong missionary, the teacher to whom he was assigned groaned. Dan thought, "The best thing we can do is to put this fellow on a plane, and send him home."

The personality conflict intensified. Dan reasoned, "If he cannot get along with his language teachers or his fellow missionaries, he surely will never be accepted by the people he is here to minister to." However, it is a serious matter to send a missionary home; after all, the fellow had not absconded with funds, nor was he guilty of immorality. Nevertheless, Dan thought he simply was not going to make it; he was not missionary material. Dan was praying that he could find some legitimate reason to send the neophyte missionary home.

One morning, during his devotions, Dan came across Romans 14:4, “Who are you to judge someone else’s servant? To his own master he stands or falls. And he will stand, for God is able to make him stand.”

Dan was stunned. It was as though God had said, “Hey, look! Here you have been praying for this person to fail, and I am praying that he will make it. I am able to make him stand.”

Dan dropped to his knees, repented for not seeking God’s wisdom and direction, and poured out his heart for the work of God in the life of the uncooperative language student.

And God answered.

The student went on to become a much loved missionary church planter.

“So then, each of us will give an account of himself to God. Therefore let us stop passing judgment on one another” (Romans 14:12-13).

Sometimes God does not merely say, “Yes,” “No,” or “Wait awhile;” although these are often true. It has been observed that there are more than 100 verses in the Bible in which God said, “I will not hear your prayer.” One such verse is Isaiah 1:15, “When you spread out your hands in prayer, I will hide my eyes from you; even if you offer many prayers, I will not listen.” Another is Jeremiah 7:16, “...I will not listen to you.”

SECTION C

Little Things

20

A Toddler Talks to God[7]

England

Joy tucked her two children into the rickety pram[8] to take them to the supermarket. Hurriedly crossing a busy street, she accidentally rammed the curb and bent a front wheel out of shape. She placed an ad on the community bulletin board in the store, "Wanted: one pram wheel," and gave her telephone number.

At home, Joy put the baby to bed and started doing the laundry. Three-year-old Kathy, however, went into her bedroom to pray for a pram wheel. In the laundry room, Joy failed to hear the telephone. Kathy jumped up from her knees and answered it.

"Honey," said a man's voice, "tell your mother I have a pram wheel for her.

Without answering, the stunned little girl dropped the telephone and yelled, "Mommie, it's Dod!" ["Dod" is toddler talk for "God."]

When Joy picked up the phone, the man, laughing, said, "I've been called a lot of things in my life, but that's a first!"

[7]Contributed by Mrs. Marguerite Peer, Kathy's grandmother; all rights reserved.

[8]pram (British): baby carriage, baby buggy

21

Monkey Business

Venezuela

"Lord, help my monkey; heal him, and help him to live for four more days." Alan was praying at the breakfast table, and he was obviously more concerned about his pet than he was about the blessing on the food.

His dad, Reverend Michael Pocock, a missionary in Venezuela with The Evangelical Alliance Mission (TEAM), was rather surprised that Alan asked that the monkey live specifically for four days, but he said nothing. He had brought the monkey home to his two boys from the interior after a hunting trip following a week of meetings.

Of course, the two boys were thrilled when they awoke and found that their father had brought them a real live monkey. Everybody enjoyed having the little critter around, but he did make an awful mess throwing things out of his cage. The first night they had him, they put him outside. When they brought him in the next morning, he looked stiff, sick and ready to die. The boys were stricken when they saw their pet in trouble. This was the cause of Alan's prayer.

By eleven o'clock that morning, the monkey was well and as active as ever. The family enjoyed his antics for several days. On the fourth day, he escaped from his cage, climbed out onto the bushes and into the trees. He fell from a tree and was killed by a neighbor's dog.

Again the boys were plunged into despair, but immediately their dad recalled that Alan had asked the Lord to let the monkey live for four days. He called his son aside and said, "Alan, why did you ask the Lord to make him live for just four days?"

"Because," said Alan, "I didn't want to be greedy."

"That was a praiseworthy motive, I suppose," said Michael when he related the story. "One thing I'm sure of—Alan never forgot that God answers prayer specifically. Many times he has benefited from what he learned on that occasion."

22

Knee Action

Alberta

Jim and Pat Riddell, while on home assignment from their mission field in Peru, had been reading some of these stories to their two daughters during family devotions.

Home assignment had been particularly trying, although the Riddells took each day as from the Lord. First, Jim had to have by-pass heart surgery. Then, he twisted his bad knee, which was weak from an earlier injury. The first doctor who examined the knee advised Jim to see a doctor who specialized in knee surgery. The earliest Jim could get an appointment was March 21. This would delay their plans to return to the field.

After reading the story, "Monkey Business" (number 21), Pat prayed specifically, "Lord, in Your will, provide a way for Jim to have a visit with the surgeon, perhaps by the end of January, so that he may have an assessment and move toward full recovery. On Monday, January 29, the surgeon's secretary called to say that there was a time open for Jim's appointment on January 31.

The assessment on January 31 led to a day surgery as soon as it was possible.

Jim comments, "Yes, He prompts us to ask specifically and to trust Him."

23

A Pampered Child

Brazil

Some say we should not bother God with little things. But are there any little or big things with an omnipresent, omnipotent God? Does an omniscient God get "bothered" when we come with sincere prayer for the things that matter to us? We tend to see our infinite God in the role of a finite parent who might reply to a child's request with, "Don't bug me now; I'm busy!" Not so with Vicki Sharp, a missionary with Unevangelized Fields Mission in Brazil and a mother of two small children.

Often the daily problems cause the greatest frustrations, especially when far from home in a strange culture and difficult climate. Preparing to return home for their first furlough, Larry and Vicki Sharp planned a ten or eleven week trip through the Caribbean.

They wanted to visit TransWorld Radio in Bonaire, Vicki's aunt and uncle in missionary service in Dominican Republic, and Unevangelized Fields Mission's work in Haiti. Traveling in rather primitive, hot countries with two small children is a chore at best, but when one of them is still in diapers, the problem is magnified. Vicki thought it would be nice to have Pampers for their youngest, Torrey. They hadn't been able to get them in Brazil, but Vicki thought, "I'm going to pray for Pampers. Just a few, just enough to get us to a place that sells them." For all she knew, that might be Miami, Florida.

Larry admits that he ridiculed the idea. "Look," he chided, "there's no sense in praying for something that's impossible. They don't make Pampers in Brazil. They don't exist here. Anybody who brought Pampers with them has used them up long ago, and no one is going to send them in the mail. Don't waste your time."

But Vicki wanted Pampers, so Vicki prayed for Pampers.

A few days later, without anyone having mentioned the matter, the lady next door came over. "I've just been sorting through my barrels," she said, "and I found a dozen Pampers, and thought you could use them. They will last you until you get to Bonaire. We've visited there, and I know they have Pampers."

24

The Rocking Chair

Illinois

Mora Bundy had always wanted a rocking chair, but for a long time such a luxury was out of the question. Her husband was in seminary, and she was working to help them financially, something she liked to call her Ph.T. (*Putting Hubby Through*) degree. When Craig graduated from seminary, he bought her a beautiful rocking chair to say, "Thank you for working so hard during these months of schooling." It was a very special chair to Mora for two reasons: (1) She had waited so long for it, and (2) it represented their united effort.

When the Bundys were appointed as missionaries to Argentina with the Christian and Missionary Alliance, many of their possessions had to be sold. Of course, the rocking chair was hardly a practical thing to pack and ship from Chicago to South America. If only they could send it to Mora's parents in Regina, Saskatchewan, or to Craig's parents in Seattle, Washington, then they could enjoy it when they were on home assignment. But there was no way. Crating and shipping it to either home was as out of the question as transporting it to Argentina.

As the time drew near to leave, Craig kept asking Mora what she wanted to do with the chair.

"We'll take it to Regina," was her answer.

"But you know we have a Dodge Colt," Craig reminded her, "and that chair is bigger than the car! There is no way in the world we can take it to Regina." But Mora knew that God was going to take care of it somehow.

Two days before departure, their pastor called on the telephone. His sister and brother-in-law were visiting him from Regina. They were driving back the next day with a new, empty station wagon. Did Craig and Mora have anything they wanted to send along?

Craig hung up the phone and joined Mora in a praise session.

25

Just A Stamp

Alberta

All Bob needed was a stamp, but he needed it urgently. Was God interested in such a little matter?

Married students with families get special attention in Bible college—not necessarily from the college faculty—but from God on a personal basis! It works like this: The Bible college provides courses in Bible, theology, Church history, music, New Testament Greek and many more subjects, but the Lord Himself schedules His own personal training in one vital course—Faith! Not that single students do not take the required course sooner or later, but the circumstances of married students often put it in the *Urgent* category. And like every course, it has its test.

Bob and Toni DeRidder ran out of money during Bob's sophomore year. They were not suffering, not running low on necessities. They just did not have any money. Well, to get technical, they did have two cents left, but that would not buy even a postage stamp! And Bob needed a stamp. He had filled out an application for a summer pastorate, but had no stamp to mail it. Several days passed, but they still didn't have a stamp or money to buy one, so they started praying for one.

Some people say that it's foolish to bother God with such little things. But perhaps the word *bother* applies to people with limitations, not to God.

The day after Bob and Toni started praying for a stamp, they received a letter from a lady to whom Toni had written recently. She said, "Your letter went through the canceling machine crooked, and it didn't cancel the stamp, so I'm sending it back to you." Hadn't God said in John 14:14, "You may ask me for anything in my name, and I will do it"?

But there was no stamp in the letter.

Sure, they were disappointed. No one had ever sent them a *stamp* before, and it seemed at first like it should have been the answer to their prayer. But on second thought, they realized they could not have used the stamp if it had been in the letter. One letter had already been delivered on that stamp. To use it again would be to take something that did not honestly belong to them. Back to prayer they went.

Soon afterwards, a letter from Mom in the U.S. arrived. Letters from Mom were always welcome, but none more than the one that came with a whole book of Canadian four-cent stamps. She had found them at the bottom of a drawer, brown with age but perfectly good. One stamp of that vintage would not have sufficed for postage even at that time, so the Lord sent a book of them!

26

The Lost Suitcase

Malaysia

Marvin and Miriam Dunn believed in talking over the ordinary details of life with the Lord, so when they retired from active missionary service in Asia, they prayed that their luggage would reach its destination safely. Leaving Kuala Lumpur, Malaysia, they rattled north by train to Bankok then flew to Switzerland for a few beauty-filled days with friends. At Zurich Airport they saw the luggage loaded on the plane for England and committed it to the Lord for safekeeping.

At Heathrow Airport later that day, they collected their bags and put them on the conveyor belt. Somehow, when they reached the bottom of the stairs, one small case with all the things needed for immediate use was missing. Inquiries produced no results and their concern was heightened by the realization that they had failed to lock the case in Zurich that morning. Marvin and Miriam put a note on their prayer list and asked the Lord to bring the case to them.

During four weeks of visiting and business in England, there was never a trace of the missing suitcase, so they quit praying. Apparently, God's answer this time was, "No."

The next stop was Three Hills, Alberta, to take part in the Overseas Missionary Fellowship's seminar at Prairie Bible Institute. On their first afternoon there, Ray and Helen Frame, furloughing missionaries, handed them their lost suitcase. Opening it, they found the contents exactly as they had packed them: Marvin's shirts, a small transistor radio, nylons and toothpaste—all there!

A taxi driver at Heathrow, when loading luggage for his passengers, had picked up the Dunns' suitcase by mistake. When the extra piece was discovered at the hotel, the driver handed it in at the nearest police station. The police kept it and waited for an inquiry. After several weeks they opened it, discovered an address inside and contacted the Overseas Missionary Fellowship's London office. Someone collected it and gave it to a lady returning to Canada. She gave it to a girl who was driving west to Briercrest Bible Institute in Saskatchewan. The young lady gave it to Ray and Helen Frame, who delivered it in person to the Dunns.

God's final answer was not, "No." It was, "Yes, I care enough about you to hear your prayers about little things." Beside the note on their prayer list, Marvin and Miriam put a big check mark and "P.T.L." (Praise the Lord).

27

Look Up!

Indonesia

Tom was stumped. He desperately needed a piece of cable to set up a generator unit to support several missions organizations, and there did not appear to be one in the entire island.

Irian Jaya, was only one of several mission fields Tom Marks visited in the summers during his student days at Prairie Bible Institute. Tom and his wife Barbara knew during their first year of Bible college in Alberta, Canada, that God was definitely leading them to Iran, and they also knew that classroom instruction was only the starting point of their missionary training. The first major lesson they would need to learn was to walk by faith.

Tom's qualifications as a first-class electrician and a carpenter put his services in demand on various mission fields When he heard of the need for someone to set up a power plant for a missionary children's school in Irian, Tom knew the Lord was pointing him there for the summer. The generator unit had been on hand for nearly two years. It would not only serve The Christian and Missionary Alliance, but also The

Evangelical Alliance Mission, Region Beyond Missionary Union, The Unevangelized Fields Mission, Baptist missions, and several little Dutch missionary societies. They all had property needing electricity. Barbara went home to Minnesota with their daughter Amber for the summer. Together, Tom and Barbara would trust the Lord to put food on their table the following school year.

"I was starting to run some distribution lines after I got the generators wired together," says Tom, "and I was running two spans to one side of a particular pole. With the heavy weight of the long spans pulling from one side of the pole, it was obvious that I needed a guy wire to pull back on the pole so it would hold up under the stress. I was wondering where we would get a thirty-five-foot piece of cable."

"We went to the largest city, Jayapura, a city of about 100,000 people at that time," Tom stated, "but there was not any technical equipment to speak of—no cable or anything like it. The nearest place to get cable, I was told, was Australia. It would take several weeks. In another week, I had to fly back to Minneapolis for my wife and daughter in order to return to Bible college for the beginning of the semester."

Back at the project, Tom went to his favorite place for prayer and meditation, an old unused runway built by American servicemen during World War II. "I was walking along praying," he said, "asking God what I could use, or how I could change the run so we could get by and proceed with the project. As I walked alongside the runway, I thought of all the things that might work. But I knew nothing but a piece of cable would do.

"With the runway on one side and the jungle on the other, I asked the Lord what to do. 'Lord, I know You led me here. You provided my airfare. The national helpers have done a good job. I am sure You did not bring me here to leave the job unfinished for another year all because of the lack of a thirty-five-foot piece of cable.'"

Just then, a voice inside Tom's mind seemed to say, "Look up, Tom."

"Yes, Lord, I am looking to You."

"Tom, look up."

"Lord, I have been to Jayapura, and I have done everything I know to do. I have no other place to look except to look up to You."

"No, Tom. Look *up*. *Look up!*"

At last, Tom looked up. What was that glinting in the sunlight between the foliage up in those trees? It looked like a piece of cable! He walked closer. Yes, it was a piece of cable all snarled among the branches. "I climbed up and worked for some time to get it down. Then I laid it along the side of the runway and measured it. Thirty-eight feet long!"

Tom assumed that some American soldiers during the war had tossed aside the cable when the trees were small, and when they grew, they carried it skyward on their limbs. But when a friend heard Tom's story—a friend who had worked in forestry for many years—he said, "No, trees don't grow that way. Trees grow from the top, and low limbs stay at the same height—or, if crowded and starved for sunlight, the lower ones could wither and fall off. If the cable had been thrown across the lower limbs, it would have probably fallen on the ground eventually."

The forester suggested that the cable may have been dropped from a helicopter when they came into use more in later years. But Tom said, "No, it wasn't in the tops of the trees, but twelve to fifteen feet off the ground."

Who knows how that cable—seemingly the only one on

the island—got to where Tom would see it when he needed it? It was obvious Who put it there.

After thanking the Lord, Tom paused, reflected a moment, and then--did he dare ask for more? Finally, he requested in awe: "Lord, two cable clamps, please." After all, you can't tie the ends of cable in a knot! He thought about the huge pile of leftover World War II military refuse the missionaries had gathered up to get out of the way. "Lord, open my eyes," he prayed, "and show me the clamps that You're going to give me."

Raising an old military truck wheel, he found a clamp. "Good, now Lord, we have only one more to go," Tom prayed. Opening his eyes after praying again, he spied another clamp. The project would go on. It was finished about three days before Tom had to leave.

"Just to show you how unbelieving humanity is, Tom adds, "I must also tell you that I thought maybe it was just a coincidence, so I started digging through that junk looking for a third cable clamp, which I didn't need. I thought I would put it away in case the missionaries needed one again sometime. I wasted about an hour and a half of the Lord's good time trying to find a clamp that wasn't there."

SECTION D

Praying in Christ's Authority

28

Spirit Worshippers

Thailand

Jim and Louise Morris, missionaries with Overseas Missionary Fellowship in Thailand, prayed that they would be able to live in a Pwo Karen village in Thailand, but the villagers would not allow it because the Morrises refused to participate in the annual spirit worship ceremony of the village. However, the Lord opened an opportunity for Louise to give much needed medical attention to some of the villagers. Afterwards, the villagers asked Jim and Louise to move into their village.

"How can we?" asked Jim. " We will not worship spirits."

"Oh, that's no problem now," the villagers responded. "There's a house available at the edge of the village. We'll tell the demons that you live outside the village."

So Jim and Louise lived among the Pwo Karen people on the edge of the demon-worshipping village in 1960, the year after they got married. Although the Lord answered their prayer for the first convert on Christmas Day in 1960, year after year passed with no real breakthrough.

At the OMF Field Conference in 1974, all of the north Thailand workers prayed and decided to make that the year for a prayer thrust for the Pwo Karen people, asking God to break through and cause people to turn to Christ in that society. God answered, first one, then another, and then a small group came to Christ.

In the village of Striped Creek, Jim's language helper, G.K., was unsaved.

"Jim," said G.K., "I've taught you all about our ways, our spirit worship, and why we do the things we do. Now, I want to test your Jesus way to see whether it works. I've made a deal; I've traded my little fields for some much larger fields."

"Well," replied Jim, "that sounds like a good deal!"

"Maybe," G.K. responded, "but the larger fields are demon fields. When anyone cultivates them, someone in their family dies. I'm going to plant them, and I want you to come and pray that Jesus will protect me and my family and give me a good harvest."

Jim prayed in Jesus' name, lifting up G.K.'s requests. In Jesus' name, he forbade the spirits to harm anyone or to hinder the growth of the crop. Then Jim helped G.K. with the slash-and-burn clearing of the fields.

When the villagers saw the men clearing the fields, they immediately asked them, "Who got cut?"

"Who got cut?" reiterated G.K. "What do you mean, 'Who got cut?'"

"You cut down the demons' fields. They cut people for doing that. Who got cut?"

"Nobody got cut."

"You cut down the demons' fields and nobody got cut?" They were incredulous. "You must have a very powerful God."

G.K. got a good harvest of rice, fruits and vegetables. He was elated. "Jesus is greater than the spirits!" he exclaimed.

But friends said, "No, you have to wait three years. If you get a good harvest for three years and nobody in your family is harmed, we'll believe in your Jesus." The number three constituted a valid test in their culture.

The second year, G.K. became very ill with a bleeding ulcer. His life was slipping away fast as they flew him to the hospital over one hundred miles away. In the emergency room, the doctors could not find a vein for the intravenous needle. Morrises' colleague, an intensive care nurse said, "Jim, it's too late. He's gone."

Then a Thai doctor found a vein in G.K.'s ankle and inserted the I.V. He. responded positively and immediately. In two days, G.K. was able to return to his village at Striped Creek.

For the rest of the three years, G.K.'s harvest was excellent every year, and there were no deaths in his family. Throughout the village everyone was saying, "Jesus is stronger than the spirits." Several families, including some of G.K.'s family, became believers in Jesus Christ.

Jesus declared, "All authority in heaven and on earth has been given to me" (Matthew 28:18). On that authority He gave the Great Commission to the Church to "go and make disciples of all nations" (Matthew 28:19). The Morrises did not attempt to exercise their personal power over the evil spirits, but claimed the authority of the Lord Jesus. That is simple faith. Yet, the story does not end there.

G.K. began to offer to sell things for other Christians, but he failed to give them all the money that was due them. Soon G.K. became known, not for his faith in his powerful Savior, but for his bad debts. Increasingly G.K. wanted to get money the easy way, so he began selling opium.

God had met G.K. in his simple childlike trust, but there

is always a spiritual battle. One victory does not guarantee total victory. Any compromise sets one up for defeat. Yet, the testimony of Christ still stands in Striped Creek.

Jot Thsaw, the headman of the Gsaw tribal village in Sop Lahm, a sister tribal group of the Pwo Karen, was addicted to opium. Jot sent for Jim to come to Sop Lahm. "I'm breaking with opium," he told Jim. "I want you to help me."

Jim had only one night with Jot and his tribe, but eight families became Christians in answer to his prayers. He taught them a little from the Bible and said, "Whatever you do, pray! Don't go back to the spirits for anything!"

Fifteen months later, Jim revisited Sop Lahm village. Five families were standing true to Christ. Three families, overtaken by illnesses, had gone back to worshiping spirits.

In Jesus' Parable of the Farmer, He told us that some good seed would fall by the path, some on rocky places and some among thorns (Matthew 13). Praise God for the seed that falls on good soil and produces a crop!

Jot Thsaw and another Gsaw tribesman were using elephants to pull trees out of the jungle for the Thai people who employed them. They came to a high hill that the elephants were not able to pull the logs over. Jot's coworker got down and prepared to go through his usual spirit worshiping rituals.

"No," said Jot. "I don't do that anymore. I pray to Jesus only."

The other man laughed scornfully. "Okay, but I'm going to worship the spirits."

Jot prayed to God in Jesus' name. His elephant was the smallest of the two, but it quickly pulled the log over the hill and left Jot's coworker and his elephant far behind. Later, the spirit worshiper and his elephant arrived in camp—but without the log! He told Jot, "I want the Jesus power."

Jot told him to talk to Jim, and the man invited Jim to his village where the man and his whole family received Jesus Christ into their hearts. Sop Lahm became the center of a movement to Christ. Sixty-five households in Sop Lahm were following Christ when Jim shared this story. The village was declared a model village by the Thai government, and the gospel spread to at least forty other villages from there. In some, the entire village was saved, and in others a few families believed.

The Lord Jesus gave the Great Commission on the basis that "All authority in heaven and on earth has been given to me [Jesus]" (Matthew 28:18). The gospel has the power to deliver anyone who lives in fear of evil spirits.

29

Conflicts With Native Spirituality

Northern Canada

Gary and Ardys Winger of Northern Canada Evangelical Mission (NCEM) have learned much about the power of prayer.

In chapel at Mission Headquarters in Prince Albert, Saskatchewan, Gary reminded fellow missionaries about the need to "Trust in the Lord with all your heart, and lean not on your own understanding" (Proverbs 3:5). Many times he and his wife Ardys have faced situations in which they needed God's wisdom.

The advent of the 21st Century confronted them with a challenge in a native village. They were asked to meet with a reserve[10] band council in the Big River Area and the missionaries working on that reserve. It was very intimidating to hear their accusations about things taught at Big River Bible Camp and how it conflicted with traditional native spirituality. The bandleaders threatened to refuse their kids permission to attend camp that year.

The NCEM missionaries, directors and friends prayed.

The outcome? God answered prayer! The band sent many kids to camp and even funded them.

Gary and Ardys served in the Inuit (Eskimo) village of Povungnituk (now Puvirnituq) on the shores of the Hudson's Bay for many years before he accepted the invitation to be Central Field Director working out of NCEM Headquarters. More recently, he has been promoted to the position of Assistant General Director of the Mission. Gary is a bush pilot, but has deliberately restricted his piloting in order to have the personal-contact ministries to which the Lord has called him. Constant decisions, witnessing, teaching, administrative duties, pastoral care of missionaries, and counseling such as this short story indicates demand a life of continuous prayer.

"Finally, be strong in the Lord and in his mighty power. Put on the full armor of God so that you can take your stand against the devil's schemes" (Ephesians 6:10-11).

---

[10]The term *reserve* in Canada is equivalent to *reservation* in the U.S.

30

Victory Over the Occult

Northwest Territories

The Northwest Territories government denied Bud Elford and Phil Howard permission to go to Fort Smith and teach the Indians to read and write in their own languages. The Northern Canada Evangelical Mission had requested permission to teach several language groups at their own expense, but they were denied because they were evangelicals and the country was solidly Roman Catholic. Mission members prayed about it. Maybe in God's time it could be accomplished.

Twenty years later the Government offered to fly them in, put them up in the best hotel and pay all their expenses to do the very job they had offered to do for free. Surely, this was an answer to prayer. But that is not the real story. It is only the introduction.

Bud and Phil were teaching two classes of high school graduates to read and write in their own languages so they could go home to their villages to teach others. It was a concentrated two-week course.

Elizabeth, a Christian girl from Snowdrift on the eastern arm of Great Slave Lake, was in Bud's class. Only recently saved and baptized, she was the only born-again believer the missionaries knew of in the Snowdrift village. She was eager to be able to read the Gospel of Mark, which the missionaries had recently translated into Chipewyan, but every time she tried to read in class, her eyes filled with tears. She was also having a difficult time learning to write her language.

A very small church was the only evangelical presence in Fort Smith. Bud and Phil attended there with their Indian friends. Midway through the two-week language session, a visiting missionary, Eva Nichol, spoke on occultism. After the service, Bud felt that he should talk to Elizabeth about her Indian background. Sitting down beside her, he said, "Elizabeth, have you ever renounced the Indian religion?"

"No, she replied. "I haven't."

"I think you should," he continued, "because it is part of the occult and it's sinful. God wants you to repent of it and renounce it. Even though you have not participated in it, your parents have, and it is the kind of sin that is visited upon the sons and daughters to the third and fourth generation." In a quiet prayer of renunciation, she followed his suggestion.

That Sunday night, Bud was asked to speak at church. His subject was, "Listening to the Voice of God." The next day, the two men had the opportunity to put the principle into practice. Bud said, "The Lord is impressing me that we should go over to the church." They went to the house behind the church where Eva Nichol lived.

When the two men arrived, Elizabeth was there. She seemed quite agitated.

"Oh," said Eva, "I'm so glad you came. Elizabeth has a problem."

"When I was a young girl, I couldn't walk," Elizabeth said. By the time I was eight or nine years old, I still could not walk, so I couldn't go to school. I would just lie in a hammock."

"My father and my grandfather were witch doctors. They came in one day and said, 'We're going to fix your legs, Elizabeth.' As far as I can remember, they took my legs off and took them outside. They sang over them and brought them back in and put them on. I have been able to walk ever since. But when I renounced the Indian religion the other night, I felt like my legs were coming off again. A voice said, 'Okay, you are not going to walk any more if you are going to leave us.'

"'I don't belong to you any more,' Elizabeth continued, 'I belong to Jesus.' Since then I can't walk very well, and I don't know what to do."

The missionaries said, "We will pray with you." They said simply, "Satan, she doesn't belong to you any more. She has chosen Jesus Christ. She has been forgiven her sins, and she wants to walk with Him."

Turning to Elizabeth, Eva said, "Elizabeth, you need to take a stand too, personally and explicitly against that particular healing." Elizabeth prayed and declared herself free. Then she stood up and said, "Oh, I can walk with ease!"

In class the next day, Elizabeth read her lesson from Mark's Gospel without any tears. Her ability in reading and writing Chipewyan improved so rapidly that by the end of the two weeks she had almost caught up with her classmates.

When Elizabeth returned to Snowdrift, she was able to share with her people.

31

Whatever It Takes

France

Marguerite Peer was sharing the gospel with an orthodox Jewish couple on a French train. An elderly woman, who had just come from a Bahai conference in London, persistently interfered. She went to the next compartment and returned with a man who was a Bahai leader. His opposition was relentless. Silently, Marguerite prayed, "Lord, *whatever it takes*, remove this man and let Your Word go forth unhindered."

Suddenly, the man fell dead across Marguerite's feet! She raced through the train in a vain search for a doctor. The conductor stopped the train, had a local doctor come aboard to certify the death, and notified the American Consulate to meet the train in Paris and take charge of the bereaved family. Marguerite was able to continue presenting the gospel—with the added impact of the immediacy of death and eternity.

In God's Word, enemies of the gospel were occasionally smitten by the Lord (Acts 12:21-23, Acts 13:6-11). Marguerite did not pray for the man's death, but that God would remove the false teacher opposing the gospel. God chose to do so through death.

SECTION E

Protection

32

Father's Day in August[11]

Pennsylvania

(By Congressman Joseph R. Pitts, 16th District Pennsylvania)

One day late in the Second World War, a squadron of kamikazes aimed themselves at a group of American ships as they sailed through the South Pacific. On the deck of one of those ships an Army chaplain saw the approaching Japanese planes and recognized them for what they were. Kamikazes were the most dangerous weapon the increasingly desperate Japanese had against American ships. Their pilots, prepared for suicide, flew explosive-laden planes directly into their targets. From October of 1944 to the end of the war in August of 1945, kamikazes sank 34 American ships and damaged hundreds of others. That's what the Army chaplain saw heading straight for him, and he froze.

He watched as one plane circled and tilted into a dive, and he prepared to die. But the kamikaze had chosen a different target. It flew directly over the chaplain's ship and into another that was sailing alongside it. It exploded in a ball of fire, killing hundreds and sending the ship and its passengers to the bottom of the sea. It dawned on the chaplain that his life had been spared, and he thanked God for it.

The Army chaplain was my father. My mother wrote my father that one night she awakened from sleep with the dreadful feeling that he was in great danger. She got out of bed and knelt and prayed earnestly for his safety. Dad wrote back and asked her the exact date and hour. It turned out to be exactly the day and hour he was under attack from the kamikaze! God heard and answered my mother's prayers!

It is not often that a man knows he is about to die and then realizes he is wrong. But that's exactly what happened to Chaplain Joseph Pitts. He had been spared, and as a man of faith, he knew he had been spared for a purpose. Through the war he witnessed the carnage and destruction of war as it worked its way through the Philippines, New Guinea and the Japanese islands. He saw the suffering, and knew that the Japanese surrender on August 24, 1945, was not really the end of it. The effects of bombs and torture and prison camps would go on for years.

After the war, my father's prayers for guidance were answered, and he returned to the Philippines with his family as a missionary. I was 8 years old. We spent several years in the Philippines, and the story of the kamikaze attack was one my father told us many times. Because of that story, I never questioned why we were there and not at home in America. I knew that my dad's life had a purpose, and that gave my life a purpose too.

Years later, an Air Force captain came home on leave after his third rotation in Vietnam. He had been in the Air Force for six years, flying more than 100 bombing missions over enemy territory. For years he had lived in places like

Thailand, Okinawa and Guam. He had seldom been home, and he had seldom seen his family. After landing, he met his wife and three children on the runway, happy to see them after so many months away. But his son, the youngest of his children, didn't recognize him. In his mother's arms, the boy smiled awkwardly and then hid his face.

I was that Air Force captain, and the year was 1968. The boy was my son Dan. I decided at that moment that I had been away long enough. At the next opportunity, I got out of the Air Force and returned to Pennsylvania to teach. From that time on, I spent as much time with my children as I could. I learned important lessons from my father and was determined to pass them on to my children too.

I taught for a few more years, and then ran for the state legislature where I served for many more years. Once again, I was frequently away from home. But I called my children every night I was away and spoke to each one about their day. On weekends, I spent special time with each of them. Once a month, I would take one of the children out for breakfast and share with them what was on my heart and listen to them tell what was on theirs. I tried to be every bit as good a father to them as my father had been to me.

Now it's Dan's turn. A couple of years ago Dan got married, and now he and his wife Paige are expecting their first child. We don't know yet whether they'll have a boy or a girl. Either way, sometime late in August, four generations of Pittses will celebrate our fathers.

"Listen, my sons, to a father's instruction; pay attention and gain understanding.

I give you sound learning, so do not forsake my teaching" (Proverbs 4:1).

"'Honor your father and mother —which is the first

commandment with a promise—'that it may go well with you and that you may enjoy long life on the earth'" (Ephesians 6:2-3).

33

A Missionary Pilot's Prayer

Nigeria

While flying through storm clouds over Nigeria, mission pilot Paul Haken told me about some of his prayer experiences.

"Many of our answers to prayer," he said, "are not in spectacular, miraculous happenings, but in everyday protection and blessings of the Lord." Each day's work is begun with prayer. When flying a small plane over hundreds of miles of bush country every day, through tropical storms in one season and harmattan dust blowing in from the Sahara in another, reminders of the good hand of God are frequent.

For instance, one day Paul's flight schedule called for take-offs at Jos and landings at Keffi and Lagos. Jos and Lagos have international airports, but Keffi has only a short landing strip for small planes. A last-minute change in the flight plan sent Paul directly to Lagos without going by way of Keffi. Upon landing, the left brake did not respond. A hydraulic line high up in the wheel well had worn, and the resultant loss of hydraulic fluid left the plane with no brake on that side. Had the plane landed on the short Keffi strip, there would have been no way to avoid an accident at high speed, but in Lagos there was plenty of room to slow down without brakes.

In another incident at Kaduna, Paul had to make another potentially dangerous landing. He had seen blue smoke pouring from the left engine of the Piper Aztec and could feel that it was running rough. A glance at the gauge revealed that the oil level was low. The only possible course of action was to shut down that engine and go in with only one. As Paul made the landing, a fire truck and an ambulance were alongside the runway waiting in case anything went wrong.

Paul managed the landing, and prepared to go to Jos where an engine overhaul would be possible. There was usually a problem getting oil at Kaduna, but this time it was available. Paul filled the engine to its normal twelve-quart capacity and a bit more. When he took off to return to Jos, blue smoke and a low oil gauge confirmed that oil was continuing to diminish. Suddenly, the engine's running smoothed out and the drop in oil level slowed dramatically. Paul continued on to Jos with no more trouble. An engine overhaul revealed a broken ring. Although SIMAir's planes undergo standard checkups by expert missionary mechanics at regular intervals, failures can occur. Mechanics and pilots alike look to the Lord for protection.

Sometimes the pilots and their airplanes are themselves the answer to someone's prayer. Paul was flying schoolchildren from Kent Academy to their parents' mission stations for vacation when he received an emergency message en route. He was ordered to go on from Egbe to Gurai near the Benin/Nigeria border to pick up a very ill patient, Missionary Pat "Pixie" Pixenberger who had the highly contagious and deadly Lassa Fever. (See story four, Lassa Fever!)

At Egbe he received word that the patient was too ill to travel from Bimbereke Hospital in Benin to the Gurai airstrip. Paul, therefore, was ordered to return to Jos for serum, which had the antibodies to counteract the virus. By the time he arrived at Gurai with the serum, he was told that it was too late and that Pat could not possibly live. However, two months later Paul rejoiced to see her recovered and going home for a rest.

34

Holdup!

Ethiopia

Peter and Brigitta Conlan, along with their coworker Peter Holmes, had decided to take a daytrip for some rest and recreation. Their job in Operation Mobilization was to make arrangements for the visit of the *M.V. Logos* ship to Ethiopia, but early one morning they started out in the Land Rover to explore some hot springs they had heard about.

Because of the famine through the Rift Valley and across North-Central Africa, they took food in case they met some destitute people. However, they had been warned to avoid any contact with the fierce Danakil tribe that had been forced out of their area by the famine. They were known to rob and kill.

Most of the day was uneventful. They saw a few lion tracks and a lot of animals that had died from the famine, nothing more. In the afternoon, they located a small village of hungry, naked people who were so desperate for food that they fought over the supplies the small missionary party brought.

On the return trip, about 50 km (31 mi.) from a paved road, the U-bolt on one of the springs under the Land Rover sheared, and one end of the spring dropped. Held up by only one U-bolt at the other end, the spring dug deep into the ground. The vehicle could not move forward. No one in the trio was a mechanic, the sun was setting, and they were in lion—and quite possibly Danakil—country.

The group started praying and hunting for something with which to loosen the good U-bolt. Jackals wandered around. Huge turtles, three feet high, came out. With no tools, they loosened the U-bolt nuts and removed the spring.

Now the Land Rover sat askew at a forty-five degree angle, so Peter and Brigitta sat on the high side out on the fender as Holmes drove. They were able to go about ten to fifteen kilometers per hour down the rough trail. It was almost dark.

Suddenly, three Danakils appeared with guns leveled at the hapless party. Peter pushed Brigitta inside the car and approached the gunman in front of the vehicle. The other two Danakils rushed to the sides of the car, opened its doors and began ransacking everything in sight. Peter walked toward the one in front and with a threatening gesture, yelled, "You move out of the way!" In response, the Danakil whipped out a long, curved knife and laid it against Peter's throat.

Brigitta, expecting to see her husband's throat slit, prayed fervently, and Peter thought, "Lord, what are we doing out here in the middle of nowhere? We've been married such a short time and now we are going to be killed!" It was not as though they were on an evangelistic trip about to die in a blaze of glory. They were merely taking a holiday, and he thought, "Lord, this is no way to end; we're just beginning our ministry."

An inner voice seemed to direct him to climb on top of

the Land Rover. From there he looked down the trail and started waving as though he recognized someone. The tribesmen stopped pillaging and looked at Peter and then down the trail. Peter waved and pointed at the robbers with signs to indicate a truck was coming. The two younger thieves, about twenty years old, talked agitatedly, and then took off running. The third, nearer fifty and perhaps the father of the others, did not appear to believe there was anyone down the trail and kept plundering. Peter jumped inside, covered Brigitta's head from possible gunshot range and told Holmes to step on it. Off they went, almost pulling the Danakil's arm off because he still had it in the doorway.

The Land Rover's lights went out after a few minutes, leaving them in utter darkness. Then, at the bottom of a dried-up riverbed, the engine stopped. They prayed and pushed, but Holmes said, "We are going to spend the night here."

"We are dead if we do," replied Peter. As if Danakils and prowling animals were not enough, the mosquitoes swarmed. Not too sure about the theology of laying hands on vehicles, the trio nevertheless did so as they prayed again. Immediately, the engine caught, and they managed to climb the incline.

By the time they maneuvered to a fork in the track, the lights started working a little. With no knowledge of where either track led, they prayed and chose one. Around midnight they reached the main highway.

A passing lorry (truck) from Djibouti stopped, and the driver towed the crippled Land Rover into Awash Village. The next morning, Peter reported the incident to the chief of police.

"You should be dead," the policeman retorted. "Two months ago an American out there was killed by Danakils. Why didn't they kill you?"

"Because we prayed," answered Peter. "Because our God answers prayer."

The policeman responded, "I know about your God. I went to a mission school."

Several months later in England, Peter's friend Johnny told him, "Several months ago I awoke about two in the morning and prayed. God laid it on my heart to pray for you and Brigitta. I did not know where you were—just in some distant country with OM. But I have never before had such a burden to pray for you like this. The next day, a strange thing happened. At our Bible study I met _______ [a mutual friend], who said, 'You know, Johnny, last night the Lord woke me at two in the morning and burdened my heart to pray for Peter and Brigitta Conlan.' We wrote to George Verwer, Director of OM to find out where you were at that time."

From Peter they learned the rest of the story. They were praying at the exact moment their missionary friends were being held at gunpoint.

35

It's in the Timing

Brazil

Larry Sharp dreaded the thought of going from church to church to present the nature and needs of their forthcoming missionary service. Although a teacher and an administrator, he had no love for public speaking. But that is exactly what he had to do as he and his wife Vicki prepared to go to Brazil for their first term of missionary service.

By mid-March the minimum support goal set by the Mission (UFM) for the Sharps seemed within reach. They lacked only $30 per month in pledged support. Vicki's pregnancy was pushing them toward a deadline. The baby was due in June and she should not travel by air after April. The Mission's director called from Alberta to Mission Headquarters in Philadelphia and told them to proceed with their plans and trust the Lord for the $30 per month as they were en route. Headquarters would go ahead with the visa applications for Brazil.

Several airlines in the United States had a special offer to attract tourists. Travelers from outside the USA could fly anywhere in the United States with any number of stops for twenty-one days on the cooperating airlines for only $150. What a blessing for young missionaries in 1972! From Seattle to Alaska for a quick visit to Vicki's parents; then to Denver, where a Christian couple said, "We will make up the total. We'll give the $30 a month." Flying into Philadelphia on the twenty-first day, they were elated over the Lord's provision for their full support—or so they thought.

At the first meeting of the UFM administrators, the Sharps learned that the Brazilian office of the Mission had requested that all new missionaries have an increase in support. For the Sharps it amounted to a staggering $90 per month more before they could leave! It was April. Vicki was nearly seven months pregnant. They knew no one on the East Coast and had no church contacts there. Time was running out.

Since Larry is Canadian, someone suggested they visit the Canadian office in Toronto. They had been excused from going that way, because it was so far out of the way from Alberta to Philadelphia. The Toronto office gave them the name of a church that would be interested in hearing them. As they traveled they discussed what their next step should be if the way to Brazil failed to open. Perhaps Larry could return to Alaska to help his father-in-law in his commercial fishing business but to do so would mean more loss of money and time. They had no peace about it, so they committed the whole matter to the Lord.

After a week in Toronto, the Sharps headed back to Philadelphia in their rented car. "Lord," they prayed as they drove, "please show us what You want us to do now."

Walking up the steps to the Headquarters building about 7:00 that evening, they were accosted by someone rushing excitedly out the door, "You've just had a call from Toronto, and they want you to return the call."

The church where they had just left wanted them to return to Toronto. They thought, "Well, that's a long way up there; they are probably interested in helping us with fifteen or twenty dollars a month, and we need ninety!" However, they rented the car again and started the ten-hour trip.

The church assumed responsibility for $75 per month and a lady in the congregation promised the other $15. It was the Lord's timing for them to become missionaries in Brazil. Little Tammy was born less than two months later.

36

Crucita Faces Revolutionaries

Honduras

"Unlock the door. Pull out that spike," demanded nineteen-year-old Crucita. "Let me out, right away, Joy. Do it *now*!"

A gang of revolutionaries at Joy Ridderhof's door was screaming to come in and take the girls that were under her care. A vicious spirit of hate and lust pervaded the atmosphere. Although Honduras was the banana center of Central America, it was also the poorest and least-developed country, as well as a land of revolutions. Much persecution was directed against Joy and the believers. Until she arrived, no missionary had been there. There was a little chapel, that had been unopened for years, and a few Christians.

One day a huge horde of Costenias came from the north coast. They were notorious for joining revolutions, not for political reasons, but for crime. Many parents in the village took their daughters to Joy for protection.

"Hardly more than a girl myself," Joy related to me, "there I was. They pushed them through the door, and it was my responsibility to protect them. The girls were in great danger from the lust-crazed revolutionaries."

"One night the whole gang arrived at the door of the mission house," said Joy. "It was a wood door that locked only with a big nail stuck into a hole. They were yelling that they must come in, they would come in, and if we did not open that door, they would break their way in. They were such wild men, and I didn't know what to do. I just could not bear to think of those girls ruined by those wicked men."

Crucita, whose name means "Little Cross," was Joy's helper. She had been gloriously saved from a tough life, and she had become a great help in the work. She had learned to read exceptionally well, and she played the little organ for the services when Joy held Bible studies or preached to the unsaved.

"Open the door, Joy!" Crucita demanded. Joy cringed at the thought of letting her out to face that mob of lustful men, but she felt she had to do it to protect the other girls. Quickly, she opened the door. Crucita stepped out. Joy, as quickly, locked the door again.

"Where's your general?" Crucita insisted. "Where's your general?"

Not waiting for an answer, she marched straight through the middle of the crowd. They were too shocked to stop her. No one laid a hand on her. Making a beeline down the street, she headed to the market place and found the general. He turned out to be the man who lived across the street from the mission house. Immediately he came and dispersed the troops, and they did not return.

"An answer to prayer?" asked Joy as she related the story. "Well, I can tell you, we were surely praying as Crucita walked down that street!"

Some years after this incident, Joy Ridderhof founded Gospel Recordings, a ministry that allowed people to listen to the gospel in their own languages, even their own accents and local idioms. Joy became known around the world for her vision and active leadership through this ministry.

37

Terror By Night

Nigeria

"My blood ran cold when I turned on the light. Right in front of me stood a stranger. He had followed me into my house."

Linda Klassen, hostess at the SIM Guest House in Kano, Nigeria, had rushed into her house at ten-thirty one evening to prepare a few things before guests arrived on a plane. Little did she know that she had not come home alone.

"What's your name?" he demanded.

"What do you want?" she asked. "Please get out of here."

He stood there, and Linda screamed.

He turned out the light, and Linda screamed again.

Sensing that he was coming toward her in the dark, she screamed yet again. Then she was on the floor. His hands were tightening around her throat. He threatened her with a knife.

"Suddenly a wonderful peace came over me," she remembered later. "I relaxed and prayed out loud: 'Dear Jesus, I know You are here and I love You, and this man needs You.'"

Immediately, his grip around her throat loosened; the door

opened. The attacker jumped up and fled. Linda's coworker Frieda Janzen had been passing nearby when Linda screamed, but she did not realize where the screams were coming from. In fact, they were almost drowned out by the many noises of the city. At first, she had gone on her way without concern. But a moment later, she felt an urge to go back and check on Linda.

38

Car on the Tracks

Alberta

A mournful whistle pierced the winter air as the Issler family tried in vain to get their van off the train tracks. Elsie and her parents were going to town in Leduc, Alberta. Right on the tracks, the van had stalled. All Dad Issler's attempts would not budge the van. Every effort was useless as the sound of the whistle came closer and closer.

Everyone was thinking about jumping out, Elsie recalls. "I could hear both my father and my mother softly asking God to help us," remembers Elsie. "'Please move the van,' they prayed. The train was no more than a quarter of a mile away when the van started to roll. Just clear of the tracks, it stopped. After a few more tries, my father started the van again."

"The Lord really made me realize in those few minutes that He could take us at any time—whether through death or the Lord's coming. We should always be ready. I also learned to trust Him more, because He can do all things if we have faith."

SECTION F

Provision

39

A No-Debt Policy

Pennsylvania

The farm, easily worth $200,000, would be an ideal place for Milton and Leora Eder's children's home. A Christian man had stipulated in his will that the children's home could buy his farm for $50,000 and the money was to go to missions. Furthermore, they could have up to two years to consider it.

They prayed. The policy of the children's home was not to incur debt but to trust the Lord to supply every need. There was no money on hand.

Time passed and a legacy was left to the children's home for the exact amount, $50,000. However, bills were coming due and the money was quickly used up. Milton and Leora knew that God did not want them to purchase the farm at that time.

However, within a year, when all the bills were paid and maintenance was well cared for, another legacy came in the same amount. This was obviously God's provision for the purchase of the farm.

40

The Joys of a Missionary on Home Assignment

British Columbia

The three-month home assignment has become very popular with mission societies these days. It is less expensive to charter an airplane for a large number of missionaries going home at one time than to pay individual fares. Children do not have to endure the trauma of changing schools. Yes, it solves many problems—and also creates a few. Have you ever tried to rent a house for three months?

Harold and Elma Hide felt the need to be alone with their four girls. It was the only time except Christmas holidays that they could be together as a family. Living with relatives would not be ideal. But where could they possibly find a three-bedroom house for only three months? It seemed that so many landlords refuse to rent to families with children at all. The parents prayed; the children prayed; the whole student body at Kent Academy in Nigeria prayed.

Elma's oldest sister had been like a mother to her, so the Hides asked the Lord for a place near her in Clearbrook, British Columbia. The owners of a three-bedroom house two blocks from Elma's sister decided to visit relatives in Ontario for three months. They offered Hides their home rent free and were so thankful to have someone to take care of it that they told the missionaries to use their telephone and anything else in the house.

The next furlough was across the continent in the east near Harold's parents. An ad in the paper yielded no response until they arrived in Toronto. Then a lady called to say that she was going to England for the summer and would rent her house to them, including sheets, dishes and utensils.

Before going on furlough, the girls had begged their parents to take them swimming often during the break. Knowing that the girls were embarrassed because they could not swim as well as other girls their age, Harold and Elma determined to give them lessons.

The house they rented was next door to Art and Beth Cairncross, members of a church that helped support the Hides, but the two families had not met previously. The three Cairncross girls were about the same ages as the four Hide girls, so they included them in all their outings and church activities. And they had a swimming pool!

By the time home assignment was over, the Hides' children had made good progress in swimming under their neighbors' tutelage. The Cairncross family and the Hide family became faithful prayer partners. And anytime the landlady goes to England the missionaries are welcome to rent her home.

41

Island Home

Dominican Republic

Moving from inland Dominican Republic to the southern coast meant a big change for Sig and Agnes Odland and family. They were going to the warmest, driest, most desert-like spot on the island. With three children being home-schooled by correspondence plus one preschooler, Agnes felt they needed a large house in a quiet place.

Moving and finding a suitable home is a frequent need for missionaries. Such times call for specific prayer. When Sig and Agnes have asked God for a particular type of home, He has never failed to give it to them. Although they have asked only for needs, He has given extra every time. This was no exception.

On a previous visit to the southern coast, they had been inside a home on the edge of town that was being rented by American oil workers. The house had a large yard with many trees and undeveloped space on three sides. Sig and Agnes agreed that this would be ideal, but fellow workers laughed at them. They knew what the house rented for, and they knew what a missionary's allowance was.

When the American oil workers' lease was up, they moved on and a nephew of the owner moved in. He failed to pay any rent and neglected to water and care for the yard. When the Odlands approached the owner and offered half of the previous rent, he gladly leased it to them.

42

No Collateral, Just God

Minnesota

Chuck Phelps, a missionary-evangelist with Open Air Campaigners (OAC), was broke. Like many interdenominational faith ministries, OAC does not pay salaries. Instead, each evangelist looks to the Lord to supply his needs through Christian friends who support the work. OAC's ministry focuses on preaching on street corners, in jails, in parks, at factories during lunch hours, on beaches—anywhere there are people. They are known for their use of a sketch board to attract a crowd, teaching courses on open-air evangelism at Bible colleges and winning countless souls to Christ.

Chuck's income was low when he moved his family into the Minneapolis area, but they managed to rent a farmhouse. About a year later, the owner sold the land and the house had to be moved.

"However, I'm going to move it about a mile down the road, and then you may continue to rent it," the owner stated.

The Phelps family got a tiny trailer in which they could eat their meals, spent their nights in a neighbor's basement, and waited to move back into the farmhouse. The farmhouse was jacked up, put on wheels, moved out by the road—and there it sat. Eighteen weeks later, the arrangements still had not changed. Chuck did not have enough money to rent another place and did not know what to do.

"I know just the house you should have," phoned a friend, "and I want you to go and look at it."

"Well, we'll look," replied Chuck, "but I couldn't buy a house!"

At sight of the house, Chuck knew that it was more than he had ever dared to pray for—three stories, seven bedrooms, carpeting throughout, and two garages (one that would be perfect for the specially equipped OAC van, the other with an air conditioner and furnace—ideal office space!)

He called a real estate agent and asked him to call Thorpe Real Estate Company, explain the circumstances, and ask them to drop out of the deal. He did not realize that real estate dealers would not think of doing such a thing. A week later Chuck called and asked, "Did you call Thorpe yet?"

"Uh—well, no, I just haven't," he stalled. However, he finally called.

The Thorpe agent said, "No, we have never dropped out of a deal, and we have three buyers for the house now."

Strangely, four days later, a call from Thorpe indicated a willingness to drop out if Chuck would pay the $100 spent on advertising.

With the $100 paid, Chuck did not have another cent to put toward the purchase of the house. Having heard that the state had allotted money for long-term, low-interest loans to low-income families, he drove to the First National Bank in St. Paul to apply for such a loan.

"Enough money has been allotted for about forty homes, but we have 140 applications," he was informed, "so there is hardly a chance that yours will be granted."

"Well, I'm here, so I'll just put in an application," Chuck responded.

"What do you do for a living?" asked the banker.

"I'm an evangelist."

"That's fine. With whom?"

"Open Air Campaigners."

"Never heard of it."

So Chuck explained.

"Does this organization pay your wages?" the banker inquired.

"No, they don't."

"Well, who does?"

"Really, no one."

"I don't understand."

"You see, sir, we live by faith."

"Faith?" he asked incredulously. "I've been the financial secretary for our church for twenty years, and I have never heard anything like this. We give our pastor a salary and a home. You mean you don't have that?"

"No, sir. We just trust the Lord for our needs," replied the evangelist.

"Well, I don't think there is a chance of your getting the loan, because we are looking for someone who has a steady income. I'm sure this won't go through, but I'll put it in anyway." Along with the application, Chuck left one of his monthly statements showing the individuals and churches that had contributed to his support.

A week later the banker called and asked Chuck to come to his office. He had the monthly statement in hand as he renewed the interview. "Now, these people who give to your support, what happens if they don't give you anything next month—then what?"

"Sir," explained Chuck, "we're not really depending on the people. We have always depended on the Lord, and He has never let us down yet."

Another man sitting behind the interviewer suddenly threw some papers into the air and exclaimed, "Oh, here we go on that faith stuff again!"

"I just don't understand," said the inquisitor as he shook his head. So Chuck went through it all again—how he worked for the Lord and asked the Lord to supply for his family's needs and how God did so through His people. Again, the banker said he had never heard anything like it and added, "I really hate to tell you this, but there's no hope. Your loan application won't go through."

"Well," the Lord's servant replied, "if the Lord wants us to have it, we'll have it." By this time, he was confident that God wanted to give them the house, so he had great peace as he left the bank.

Two weeks later the telephone rang. The secretary at the bank said, "Sir, your application for a loan for the purchase of a house has been approved."

About twenty-five years later, when a banker in Anoka, Minnesota (a suburb of Minneapolis) was talking to Chuck, he asked, "Chuck, do you still have that house on Fifth Avenue South?"

"Yes," replied the evangelist, "I do."

Afterward, Chuck wondered why the banker, a Christian from a Brethren Assembly and a personal friend, asked about the house. Chuck called him and invited him for lunch a few days later. There, he asked, "Why did you ask me whether I still have the house?"

"Because I was on the board that considered your loan application. When it came up, everyone just laughed, but I said, 'Let's give him a chance.'" Until then, Chuck had never known how that application had been passed.

Chuck's children are grown now, and Chuck and his wife no longer need the large house on Fifth Avenue South, but they will never forget the way the Lord provided it for them. Chuck is now a thirty-year veteran with OAC and going strong for the Lord.

43

Stingray!

Red Sea

Bruce and Norene Bond and their children traveled for three days from their SIM station in Ethiopia for the adventure of a lifetime. On the shore of the Red Sea, they piled out of the car and set up camp. Bruce and the boys hurried off to spear a fish, while Norene and Becky got out the frying pan.

"There's a big one!" someone shouted. "Come on, boys," yelled an excited Bruce, "watch your father spear supper!"

They headed for what appeared to be a huge fish churning in shallow place, presumably trying to find deeper water as the tide receded. Bruce hefted the beautifully balanced shaft and hurled it. All watched as the point sank with a rewarding thud.

But before it could be captured, the intended supper flapped furiously over a sand bar and escaped.

"It's a stingray!" the boys shouted in dismay. "And he's taking the spear with him!"

"Oh, well," one of the boys said, "we wanted a real fish anyway, not a stingray."

"But the spear!" another groaned. "It's not ours!"

The Bonds had accepted the loan of the beautiful, handmade spear reluctantly when a missionary friend insisted that they take it along. Such an expensive, hand-made instrument would be almost impossible to replace.

Lying in their sleeping bags on the sand that night, after a supper of beans, the family prayed together. "Daddy," asked little Becky, "can't we ask God to give us back our spear?"

Parents who teach their children that God answers prayer sometimes are put to the test. With weak faith, but unable to remove themselves from the corner Becky had backed them into, they asked God to send the spear back and dropped off to sleep.

Strolling on the sandy beach early the next morning, Bruce half hoped to see the spear washed ashore. But there was no spear. During family prayers after breakfast Becky again reminded them to pray for the spear. Bruce, with his enthusiasm for water sports mostly gone, watched camp while the others went swimming in the tropical water.

"Stingray!" the cry went up, "Dad, a stingray!"

Bruce was unimpressed. He had seen enough stingrays for one holiday.

"Dad!" The cry persisted. "It's the one with the spear!"

Bruce leaped into action. Quickly, he tied a large fishhook to a long pole. Sixteen hours since the thing had swum away—with the whole Red Sea to disappear into—and it was back again!

It swam gracefully close to shore and after a few attempts Bruce felt the hook sink into the wooden shaft. A firm tug released the spear, and the stingray sped out to sea. God had made the axhead swim for Elisha; now He made an iron spear swim right out of the Red Sea into Bruce Bond's hands.

Becky proclaimed triumphantly, "God does answer prayer, doesn't He?"

44

The Other Ninety

Indiana

Pappy Reveal was quite a man. If you had gotten the chance to hear him speak, you would never forget it. Pappy had long been a favorite Bible conference speaker for thousands of Christians. Although he was crippled by an accident in his youth and walked with braces on both legs and two canes in his hands, nothing would stop him. He directed camps and ran homes for children, unwed mothers and abused women. Where there was a need, he accepted it as his responsibility and proceeded by faith to do something about it.

The dynamic little white-haired Director of the Evansville Rescue Mission (Evansville, IN) talked to God so intimately and frequently, even in the midst of his sermons, that one often failed to detect just where the preaching took a recess and the praying took over. But it was not at all difficult to recognize the unique closing he always used for his prayers. "Amen, Lord, amen," he piped in his cheerful, boyish tenor.

One day the rescue mission had a bill due for $100 and no money to pay it. (In the 1940's $100 was equivalent to a couple of thousand dollars today!) Pappy's mission staff prayed about the bill during their daily prayer meeting right after lunch. Because of his crippled legs in unbending braces, Pappy stood while the others knelt. He laid his canes aside, put his hands behind his back and rocked back and forth as he prayed.

A friend passing the mission looked in through the large plate glass window and saw Pappy's fingers opening and closing as he rocked and prayed. Thinking he would have a little fun, the young man tiptoed in without a sound and slipped a crisp $10 bill between Pappy's grasping fingers. Without a break in the rhythm of his swaying and praying, Pappy swept his hand around in front of his face, threw the ten spot down on the chair in front of him, and said, "Thank You, Lord! Now, where's the other ninety?" After that, he continued praying and opening and closing his hands behind his back.

The practical joker who had contributed the $10 suddenly felt an impulse to join the prayer meeting.

At one o'clock the group dispersed to various tasks, and the postman came in with a stack of mail—mostly magazines, junk mail and more bills. In the whole pile there was only one letter with a gift for the mission—a check for $90!

The practical joker was amazed to discover that God was precisely directing his actions, even when he was engaged in something as insignificant as a joke.

45

Tomorrow Will Be Too Late!

Zaire

"Please, God send us a hot-water bottle," prayed ten-year-old Nammy. "Be no good tomorrow, God, the baby'll be dead. Please send it this afternoon."

Inimitable Dr. Helen Roseveare, Medical Missionary with WEC Int., tells the story with rapid-fire oratory. To capture the drama of it on the printed page is nearly impossible. Dr. Roseveare is also the author of a number of books[12] and has this story in several of them, but she gave me permission to borrow it from a tape-recording made of a message she gave at the Prairie Bible Institute Missions Conference. To edit out her British vernacular (colloquialisms, idioms, etc.) would be to destroy its uniqueness, so every effort has been made to capture it in print as closely as possible. This incident occurred in Zaire, at that time called Belgian Congo, in Africa.

"I was called out to the maternity. We worked hard, but despite everything we could do, the woman died in childbirth, and I was left with a tiny premature baby and a little two-year-old girl orphaned by the death of her mother.

"I said to the midwives, 'Our problem is going to be, in order to keep this baby alive, to keep it at a steady temperature.'"

"We'd no incubator there, no electricity. The one nurse went out to get the boxes we put babies in and the cotton wool we wrap them in. Another midwife went out to fill the hot-water bottle. Another stoked up the fire. One of them came back in and said, 'I'm awfully sorry, Doctor, I boiled the water, I poured the water in, and suddenly—buh!' A burst hot-water bottle! And she said, 'It's the last hot-water bottle!'

"You have a saying, 'It's no good crying over spilt milk.' In Africa we might say, 'It's no good crying over a burst hot-water bottle.' They don't grow on trees, and no drug store down the road to buy another.

"I said, 'All right, you put the baby as near to the fire as you possibly can—sleep between the baby and the door. Your job is to see it does not get into drafts.'

"Next day, at midday, I was having prayers with our orphan children for any of them who wanted to gather 'round for prayer time, as I did every day. I gave them various things to pray for, and amongst the prayer requests I told them of this tiny premature baby and how difficult we were going to find it to keep the baby alive. I mentioned the burst hot-water bottle. I told them of the little two-year-old girlie who was crying because her mommy had died.

"One of the children, ten-year-old Nammy, took the matter up in prayer in the usual blunt way about African kiddies, 'Please God, send us a hot-water bottle. Be no good tomorrow, God, the baby'll be dead. Please send it this afternoon.' And then she added, 'And while You're about it, God, would you send a doll for the little girl so she'll know You really love her?'

"As always, my problem with children's prayers was—could I really say, 'Amen'? I didn't honestly believe God could do it. Oh, I know God can do everything. I love that hymn, "God of the Impossible." Of course, it's super! But I mean—there are limits, aren't there? I mean, it wasn't really possible He could cope with that one!

"I'd been out there three years. I'd never had a parcel. They just didn't come. Our mail usually came every now and again when somebody happened to be coming in the right direction. And anyway, if anybody from my home country did send me a parcel, who would put a hot-water bottle in? I was on the equator!

"Well, about midway through the afternoon, I was teaching in the Nurses' Training School, and somebody came and said, 'There's a car outside your house, Doctor.' I went across, but when I got there, the car had gone. But there on the verandah was a large 22-pound parcel, all done up with string and United Kingdom stamps. I think I felt the tears then. I couldn't open it alone. I sent for the orphan kiddies, and we opened it together.

"On the top there were lots of these bright knitted vests that they love, and I was throwing them out as their eyes lit up and just praying, 'Please, God, there must be enough vests to go 'round for everybody.' Then there was a large bar of soap, and they looked bored. And then there was a nice package of mixed fruits, and their eyes lit up. It would make a nice batch of cookies for the weekend. And then I pulled out. . .the brand new hot-water bottle. I cried.

"Nammy was in the front row of children. She rushed forward and said, 'If God sent the bottle, He must have sent the doll.' She dived into the parcel with both hands, and she pulled out the dolly. She had never doubted. She just looked up at me with bright eyes, 'Please, Mommy, may I go over with you to the maternity to give this doll to that little girl so she'll know that Jesus really loves her?'

"That parcel was on the way five months. Five months before, God had constrained a Sunday school group to put a parcel together—some Sunday school teacher to put in a hot-water bottle (even for the equator)—some child in England to put in a doll for a little one out in Africa, because God wanted to answer a child's prayer that afternoon. I tell you, He's some God, isn't He?"

---

[12]For Helen Roseveare's books, contact WEC International, Fort Washington, PA 19034.

46

No Water!

Nigeria

The words, "No water!" were ominous words. Everything depends on water. But the reservoir for the seminary of the Evangelical Churches of West Africa (ECWA) in Igbaja, Nigeria, was almost dry.

The usual rainy season from April to October should have assured a reservoir full to overflowing by the end of August, but very little water remained in it. School was to start in September.

In town water was selling for one naira, eighty kobo ($2.70 to $3.00 U.S.) per bucket. The Sudan Interior Mission (now SIM Int.) personnel and their ECWA coworkers at the seminary were united in a common cause—praying for water. In the third week of September the answer came. Rain fell in torrents. Although it was late in the season, the reservoir filled. Then the rain stopped.

SECTION G

Soul-Winning Prayer

47

One Tablet at Bedtime with a Large Dose of Prayer

Nigeria

Fulanis are a nomadic people group who roam the open country in several west African countries. They are usually cattle herders and practice the Muslim religion. They tend to be suspicious of strangers and do not usually welcome them to their encampments. Missionaries are liable to be stopped at the entrance.

Linda Klassen and her coworker learned of a sick woman in the Fulani camp. After much prayer, they were allowed to go in to see her. She was obviously very ill. Emaciated from weeks of sickness, she was suffering horrifically. Her baby, lacking mother's milk, was skin and bones.

The missionary ladies persuaded the people to let them give the woman some medicine, but all they had were a few aspirin tablets. They saturated the aspirin with prayer and prayed daily for an entrance into the Fulani camp.

A few weeks later, the missionaries stopped by the encampment, and were met with a tumultuous welcome! People poured out of the camp to meet them and invited them in. The sick woman had improved immediately after taking the aspirin, and in three days she was able to do all her regular tasks. The missionaries were able to share Christ with the Fulani people and to tell them that it was not the aspirin but Jesus who had healed her in answer to prayer.

48

Charley—A Street Boy

Philadelphia

The child looked severely malnourished. Charley's hair was falling out, and he looked like he was five or six instead of his actual age of eight. He had never known a home except with his drunken grandfather. Sometimes his grandpa let him buy a hot dog, but mostly Charley lived on the streets of Philadelphia and ate out of garbage cans. He had seldom gone to school.

The children's home superintendent called Milton and Leora Eder, who were already house parents to twelve boys: "Please have that empty bed prepared to take in another boy this afternoon."

Other than a name and the rags on his skinny frame, Charley had no possessions. Milton took him into the bathroom and cleaned him up for supper. When Leora spooned some eggs onto the waif's plate, he grabbed them with both hands and gobbled them down, almost too fast for anyone to see what had happened.

As time went on, in answer to the Eders' prayers, Charley began to understand his need for Jesus Christ as his personal

Savior and was born again. After graduation from high school, he went into the army during the Vietnam Conflict and was made Assistant Chaplain at Walter Reed Hospital. Every time the Eders received a letter, there were several Scripture verses at the bottom of the page. After the army, Charley went to Bible college and became a teacher in a Christian school.

49

The Difference One Can Make

Philippines

Every day prayer partners worldwide pray for Action International Ministries'[13] work among street children as well as their other outreaches to those with little or no opportunity to hear the gospel. This story is one of many answers to those prayers.

Jeff and Mary Ann Anderson shared this testimony of one of the street kids of Manila who trusted Christ during an ACTION (Action International Ministries) camp.

Pandacan is a very tough area in the City of Manila. Living Bread Baptist Church is located in its heart. Living Bread is a very active soul-winning church and is a regular partner of ACTION in reaching street children for Christ.

Robert Goco was invited to attend an evangelistic camp for street kids in June 1999. At that camp, Robert, who had been a hard-core drug addict, repented of his sin and believed on Jesus Christ as his Savior and Lord. He became a living witness of God's saving grace to his family, friends and neighborhood. As a result of Robert's changed life, his mother came to the next camp. There she realized that salvation was for her also, not just for white people or the rich as she thought.

Robert and his mom continued to grow in their walk with Christ, and Robert continued to invite people to camp and Living Bread Church. One couple, Edwin and Rose, were Muslims and notorious in their neighborhood as troublemakers. They also trusted Christ and are now actively serving in the church. Edwin is usually the first to arrive on Sunday mornings to help arrange the worship center. Edwin and Rose are growing in Christ and are also inviting friends and relatives to the church.

Romeo Flores, another recruit of Robert's, was a former homosexual. He is now following Christ as his Lord and Savior. Romeo has led his eighty-three-year-old grandmother, mother and three sisters to faith in Christ. Romeo is now being discipled by a church worker, is an active member of the church choir and a Sunday school teacher. Every Sunday Romeo brings people to church.

Robert, Mrs. Goco, Edwin and Romeo have continued to invite many people to church and camp, and several have come to Christ through their outreach efforts. According to Dely Velasco, a faithful partner in the ministry, "These young people are very active in the church and continue to grow in their spiritual life."

There are many more exciting reports about these young people, and it is amazing to see the way God has changed their lives. Although there are many things they need to learn yet, and they need discipleship, the Andersons see spiritual growth in the lives of the street children. They meet together every Thursday for group Bible study.

---

[13]See Action International Ministries' Web site at www.actionintl.org.

50

Last Communion

Nigeria

"I have told my wife and five children and my elderly parents goodbye for the last time. I have come this morning to have my last time in church. I came to take communion; then I am going out to kill myself," declared Patrick, a student at the teacher training college in Zaria, Nigeria.

Patrick had waited behind after the communion service when Harris Poole, missionary with SIM International, spoke in chapel at the training college. He approached Harris in the vestibule and asked if they could have some time together. They made their way back into the chapel where the student poured out his pathetic story. He had been into many kinds of sin and trouble and had gone to witch doctors, hospitals and churches to find release from his bondage. Finally, he had determined to take communion and then end it all.

"I would like to share with you what it means to really belong to God," Harris said as he shot up an "arrow prayer" to ask God for wisdom, a work of grace in the young man's heart and the right words. Then he went through the plan of salvation with him. "Have you ever truly turned your life over to Jesus and asked Him to come in?"

"No, I have not," replied the student.

"Do you want to? I know God is here," said Harris, "and He wants to help you."

With tears streaming down his cheeks, Patrick told God how sorry he was and repented of his sins. He asked God to forgive him, to be merciful to him and come in and save him.

When Patrick finished praying, Harris asked, "Now, would you like to go and commit suicide?"

"Oh, no! Not at all," Patrick replied. "God is my answer, and I am grateful."

Patrick became very active in the Fellowship of Christian Students and attended prayer meetings regularly. He continued with his studies at the Teacher Training College. He had been preparing all along to teach the Bible—yet he had not been saved! After his saving encounter with the living Lord Jesus, he was ready to teach the Bible with real meaning.

"Arrow prayers," as Dr. Helen Roseveare of WEC International calls them, are effective prayers made when our hearts are prepared and in tune with the Holy Spirit's direction. Sometimes He mercifully answers even when we aren't so prepared! Peter prayed one such when he felt himself sinking in the stormy waters and cried out, "Lord, save me!" However, if we rely solely on arrow prayers in tough situations, we are liable to push the panic button instead of truly praying.

Harris Poole had daily communion with the Lord. He and his wife prayed together and individually. Their service for God was bathed in prayer. He prayed before he went to the chapel service. He had asked the Lord for wisdom, guidance and the Lord's glory in the lives of the students. When the time came to shoot up an arrow prayer for help, he was ready and God was listening.

51

A Good Testimony

Colombia

"It is so important that we pray intelligently for missionaries—and not just with an occasional, "God bless the missionaries," but lifting up specific requests for specific needs. Often missionaries cannot share some of their most crucial needs because information put into writing, even in a prayer letter, has a way of getting into the wrong hands and creating problems. However, one essential prayer that can be said for all missionaries is to ask God to make their lives a good testimony for Him among their neighbors and business contacts.

Ed Wallen recalls three incidents when missionaries in Colombia were very aware of the prayers of folks back home. When Ed arrived in Colombia, he noticed right away that he was accepted as an honest, trustworthy person because the missionaries before him had a solid testimony. People had come to associate any evangelical missionary with an honest, upright life. As a latecomer, Ed was a recipient of that heritage and could enjoy it.

Ed was the buyer for the Bible school where he taught. He had a long list of items to purchase in bulk at one store.

The clerk who was loading the truck engaged him in conversation, so Ed wasn't paying close attention to what was being put into the truck. At the mission house, before going up the mountain to the school, he stopped to rearrange the load. It was then that he noticed he had a couple of bars of soap too many and a large box of laundry soap was missing. He returned to the store thinking, "This is useless. He will never believe me." Merchants in Colombia just do not trust people. If you have left the store when you discover that something is missing, it is just too bad. There is no way that you will get what you think you are missing.

When Ed related the errors to the manager, the man who had loaded the truck was standing nearby and said, "We gave him that box of soap." The manager turned to him and said, "These missionaries are honorable people. If they say that they didn't get the laundry soap, they didn't get it. Now, go and get the laundry soap."

The prayers of God's people at home for the testimony of the missionaries are absolutely vital. A second incident confirms this.

The national bank in Colombia was robbed of fifty million pesos, all in five hundred peso bills. The government did not catch the thieves, so they merely declared the 500-peso bill to be no longer legal tender in any store. It was required to be turned in to the national bank and exchanged for other denominations of money. The 500-peso bill was worth about $25 U.S. at that time. Ed had one to turn in, so he joined the line of about forty people in front of the bank across the street from the post office. As they waited to get in, everyone was checking the serial numbers on their bills against the posted list of stolen ones.

While he stood there, a young lady ran across the street from the post office with a hundred-peso bill in her hand, about two-and-a-half-days wages for her. She said to Ed, "We are out of change in the post office. Can you get this changed for me?"

"I'll be glad to," responded Ed, but he thought, as he looked around, "I'm the only person in this line who isn't from here; yet she picked me to get the money for her. If I should fail to return with it, they would take the money out of her wages. She recognized that I was a missionary. What a testimony the missionaries have!"

Again, coming down off the mountain road in a truck, Ed and a fellow missionary met a roadblock. The police were looking for some escaped criminals. They pulled over all the people passing that way, put them up against the truck with their hands over their heads and leveled machine guns at them. A bus and a number of cars were stopped, and the police looked through belongings for weapons or papers.

One guard said to another, "Hey, this fellow is a missionary."

Ed's companion said, "We are both missionaries."

The guard replied, "Get back in your truck and go on around." The two missionaries drove off while everyone else was detained. Being missionaries, they were above suspicion.

Answers to prayer cannot only be counted by the miraculous interventions of God. They also include continuous recognition of God's servants by the world.

52

A Poor Witness

Costa Rica

"Is Anita on duty? I want her to take care of me." It was a frequent request at the mission hospital in San Jose, Costa Rica. Anita was one of the best nurses in the community, well known, the kind who always goes the second mile.

When Anita became ill, she became a patient in the hospital where she had served so faithfully and well. The diagnosis: leukemia. It progressed to the point where doctors were saying, "It's only a matter of days until she dies."

While lying there, apparently on her deathbed, Anita communed with her Lord. The essence of her prayer was, "Lord, I have tried to be the best nurse I could be. All these years I have done what I could to take care of the bodies of my patients, but I never had real concern for the condition of their souls. Lord, if You will raise me up from this bed and get me back to nursing again, I will make sure that I do better. I'll work as I should as a nurse to help people have health in their bodies. At the same time, I will buy up every opportunity to help people have spiritual health in coming to know Jesus Christ as Lord and Savior."

A few days later, the doctor stood at Anita's bed and said, "We don't know what happened, but we have to change our diagnosis." The color began to return to Anita's face. Her strength gradually came back and she kept her promise.

Calling on Mrs. Gordon Hauser, wife of the hospital administrator, she pleaded, "Come and help me. Show me how I should approach a person. Tell me what verses I should be learning. Help me to prepare for an opportunity when it comes." As soon as her strength permitted, she and Mrs. Hauser did a lot of visiting and witnessing together. Anita spearheaded it.

Once, when a mother was leaving the hospital with twin babies, Anita said to herself, "How in the world can she take care of those babies by herself at home when she can't do it here with all the help we are giving her?"

Anita said to the mother, "May I come around to your house and help you with the babies?" The mother gladly accepted the offer, and soon Anita led her to Christ. The mother's life was so transformed that her neighbors became perturbed. They put a little sign on the front of her house intending to keep Anita from spreading her teaching. The sign said, "We don't want any kind of propaganda in this house."

When the husband came home and saw the sign, he said, "Who is trying to tell me what to do?" He tore down the sign, went in and asked his wife, "What's this all about?"

His wife gave her testimony but was unable to explain fully because it was all so new to her. "Let's get Anita and let her tell you," she suggested.

But Anita said, "No, I don't want to talk to a man." Instead, she asked Gordon Hauser to talk to him.

So the Hausers and Anita went over one evening. After the usual salutations, the women went to check on the twins and left the two men alone in the living room. Gordon was trying to think of a good approach. Verses of Scripture and various ways of leading into a conversation were running through his mind. "How should I start talking to this fellow about the Lord?" he wondered.

"All right," said the man, looking Hauser straight in the eye, "you came here to tell me something, now tell me."

In a few minutes the two men were on their knees and the man received Jesus Christ as his personal Savior and Lord. With joy overflowing, he then went to tell his wife of his newly found peace in perfect forgiveness of the Lord.

It was all in answer to the prayer of the nurse who prayed, "Lord, give me another opportunity." Have you prayed for such an opportunity?

53

He Cared About Me![14]

Argentina

Zurdo hit his wife so hard that the baby she held in her arms was sent sprawling to the floor under their bed. Petrona in turn reached for the first thing her hands could find—a lit kerosene lamp. She hurled it at his bare back with all her strength. It struck his flesh, burning him badly. But his state of drunkenness was so great that he felt no pain. Instead, he fell face down on the bed in a stupor.

Alcoholism, which ravages the lives of many millions of people around the world, completely held Zurdo and Petrona in its vicious grip. He was an excellent mason but could not keep a job for more than a couple of weeks. They lived in a filthy hovel in the town of Curuzu-Cuatia, Argentina. Their belongings were reduced to a bed, a couple of boxes, a kerosene lamp and a one-burner stove. Petrona had sold most of their household items to buy food for her and their two children.

Then God sent a ray of light into their wretched home. A fellow workman, a member of The Christian and Missionary Alliance church in Curuzu-Cuatia, met Zurdo and began to pray for him and witness to him. The pastor of the church, Reverend Adolfo Barria, began to visit him often wherever Zurdo worked.

Finally, Zurdo was persuaded to come to a worship service at the church. In response to the love and interest the two men had shown, Zurdo accepted Jesus Christ as his Savior. The changes in his life were immediate. He stopped drinking, kept his job and regularly attended the services at the church.

Amazingly, the transformation in Zurdo's life infuriated Petrona. She refused to let him bring a Bible home and said she much preferred his drunkenness to the heresy of evangelical Christians. Her vengeful and vindictive spirit made her husband's life at home almost more unbearable than before. Zurdo asked Pastor Barria to pray for his wife but told him not to go near their home. He didn't know what she would do to the pastor. The entire church began to pray for Petrona.

One day Pastor Barria felt that the Lord wanted him visit her while Zurdo was working. Asking the Lord to help him know what to say, he bravely set out. One of Petrona's children saw him coming and ran to tell her mother. The pastor's audacity so shocked her that before she could make up her mind what to do, he was at the door. Once inside the house, he greeted her courteously. She sullenly offered him a box to sit on.

To this day, Petrona is not sure what they talked about, but she dates her conversion to the time of Pastor Barria's visit to her home. Part of what pierced her hard heart was his kindness and concern. "He acted as though he cared about me," she says.

As God's love worked in their lives, the changes became evident to their friends and family. Nine members of their immediate family have found the Lord through their testimony. Zurdo leads Bible study meetings in seven different homes during the week. The couple actively visits people to tell them what God did for them.

---

[14]The Christian and Missionary Alliance: Canadian Headquarters: Box 4048, Regina, SK S4P 3R9

Immigrant family have found the Lord through their testimony. Zuhur leads Bible study meetings in seven different homes during the week. The couple actively visits people to tell them what God did for them.

Lord, Take Everything!

[illegible]

[illegible]

[illegible]

54

Lord, Take Everything!

United States

"Have Thine own way, Lord!
Have Thine own way!
Hold o'er my being
Absolute sway!
Fill with Thy Spirit
Till all shall see
Christ only, always,
Living in me!"[15]

How does God answer when these words become our prayer, when we *truly* pray them? The following story is a first person account from Dr. Stephen Olford[16] about a time when he and his wife Heather learned the answer to this question on a routine airplane flight.

Heather and I were flying to Houston for a Keswick Convention. Shortly after we took to the air in a commercial jet, a flight attendant came up and looked at Heather for a few moments and asked, "Mrs. Olford, weren't you at the piano last night at Calvary Baptist Church?"

"Yes," replied my wife, "I was."

"Well, where was your husband?"

"Oh, he has a great convention coming up in Houston, and he wanted some rest, so he had one of his colleagues take the service. But here he is."

And she looked at me and said, "You know, I've heard about you, and I want to tell you that something terrific happened to me just recently!" Her eyes were dancing.

I asked, "What is your name?"

"Cathy__________."

"And what happened to you?"

She told me that she had been brought up in a Christian home, had been taught to read the Bible from infancy, and had known what it was to go to church.

"And all that was fine," she added, "but somehow my life just didn't count for Jesus. But now, you know, something happened just a few months ago. I went to a conference and learned that the Holy Spirit could fill my life if I made Jesus undisputed Savior and Sovereign. I stood to my feet, and I said, 'Lord, You're going to take everything, everything. I'm giving You everything!' And you know, Dr. Olford, the Holy Spirit flooded my life, and I want to tell you, it's been thrilling ever since. The greatest joy of my life is that I can't help talking about it. And God called me to the most wonderful ministry—this very airline! I have a captive audience every day."

She was talking loud enough for everybody to hear her in the first few rows. I thought, 'What exuberance! What enthusiasm! How thrilling!'

She had to go and do some work, so I buried myself in my Bible and started to study. She brought a meal, and when that was over and cleared away I thought, "I'll get right back to my Bible because I've got to be preaching on arrival."

But no way! In a few moments, Cathy was back. She said, "Oh, Dr. Olford, please come. I'm having a gospel meeting at the back of the plane. There's a Catholic, a Jew, and an atheist—and there's one guy who doesn't know what he is. And I'm stuck. Please come and help me."

"I went back, and for the rest of the journey, we had a gospel meeting. I handed out tracts and my cards. I want to tell you, that girl made such an impact, I'll never forget it."

As we were leaving the plane, Cathy said, "Dr. Olford, just a moment." Handing me a business card, she asked, "I wonder if you'll phone this gentleman when you get to Houston." I saw a string of degrees after his name—a tremendous oil magnate. She added, "I witnessed to him, and I'd love for him to come to your meeting."

When I got to my motel, I phoned through a battalion of assistants and finally reached him. "Sir, you don't know me from Adam," I began, "but I was introduced to you by a card given to me by a young lady on an airline plane."

"Cathy _________!" he exclaimed.

"Right."

"Sir," he responded, "I don't know who you are, but I want to tell you that in forty semester hours of religion courses at the university, I didn't learn a single thing that young lady told me the other day. And I want to tell you right over this telephone, whatever she has, I want."

---

[15]"Have Thine Own Way, Lord!" by Adelaide A. Pollard, 1862-1934; Copyright 1907. Renewal 1935, by G. C. Stebbins. Assigned to Hope Publishing Co. All rights reserved. (Used by permission.)

[16]Stephen F. Olford, D. D., Litt.D., President, Encounter Ministries Incorporated, P. O. Box 757800, Memphis, TN 38175-7800

55

Today, People Prayed for You!

Nigeria

An exuberant Rose Roth rushed into Herb and Marcy Jones' dining room just as Marcy served dessert. No one had a chance to ask why she had not been there at the beginning of the meal with the other invited guests.

"Guess what! I've just led six of my boys to the Lord," she blurted without waiting for introductions.

Herb, Marcy and Rose were missionaries with SIM International in Omu Aran, Nigeria. Rose taught religious knowledge classes. All Nigerian school children were required to take either Christian or Muslim instruction.

For three days, the lessons in the prescribed Christian curriculum for thirteen- and fourteen-year-olds had been from John 3. Nigerians are very outspoken with questions and opinions, so Rose's classes provided her with ample opportunity to explain the new birth. Discussions led to questions about sin, Satan, the purpose of Christ's death on the cross, and the need for personal acceptance of Jesus as Savior.

As she left the classroom, two or three boys joined Rose

to ask more questions. While they were standing on the playground talking, the group increased to twelve or thirteen children.

"I want to have the new life," volunteered one.

Recognizing the possibility that he might want to win her favor in order to enhance his grade for the course, Rose questioned him thoroughly. He assured her that he really meant it, and two or three others said that they did too.

Although many Nigerian children would admit to being Christian because they were born into Christian rather than Muslim families, few of Rose's students had given evidence of being new creatures in Christ Jesus. The occurrence of several students asking to be led to Christ while other children on the playground looked on was not something that happened everyday.

"Right here on the compound?" she asked.

"Yes, I want the new birth now," they responded one by one.

So teacher and students bowed their heads. She prayed and had them repeat the prayer after her. Then she instructed each boy to clinch the matter by talking to the Lord in his own words. When they had finished, six had prayed the penitent's prayer. Some others in the group, when asked whether they wished to pray, openly said no. Rose gave the new converts verses of assurance that Satan could not take away the salvation that Christ had given them, verses they would need when taunted by classmates.

As Rose related her account at the Jones' table, Marcy suddenly exclaimed, "Do you realize that today people around the world prayed for you?" Reaching for the SIM Prayer Guide, she flipped the pages to Day 17. One of the requests listed was: "Omu Aran: Teaching Bible in Government schools."

56

I *Know* You!

Florida

Chuck and Fran Phelps' corner of the worldwide mission field is the United States. They serve by faith with Open Air Campaigners, a ministry described in story 42. No salary, no organization or denomination to underwrite their livelihood or travel and ministry expenses. They give their lives to the evangelistic ministry. God supplies their needs in answer to their prayers and the prayers of friends. Of course, God gets a bit of assistance from the friends! As in the Old Testament Levitical priesthood, God's people give to Him, and He in turn gives to His servants.

In Pahokee, Florida, a group of six teenagers from the Church of the Master Lutheran Church in Brooklyn Park, Minnesota, worked with Chuck and Fran. In one week, 500 kids were reached with the gospel message! Many responded to the invitation to trust in the Lord Jesus and many were counseled. The Minnesota team was a great help in all the meetings and personal counseling.

One afternoon they went to a fast-food restaurant. When they walked in, Chuck walked over to a teenage boy who was sitting in a booth reading a children's Bible storybook.

"Why are you reading that book?" asked the evangelist.

"I want to be able to teach other kids about Jesus," replied the boy. "I am learning these stories."

When Chuck told him that he and Fran go into housing projects where he paints illustrations of Bible stories on his sketchboard, the teenager said, "I know you. I lived in one of those projects when I was seven or eight years old."

At that, Chuck went out to their Open Air Campaigner van and got a photo album to share with his new acquaintance. Pretty soon the boy shouted, "Here I am sitting on a bike, and here I am over here in another meeting!"

What a blessing! To God be the glory! The Lord is still in the business of multiplying the Bread of Life through a boy's lunch.

Chuck and Fran could not do this work without the prayers and support of friends. They are grateful for each one who has such a vital part in this ministry.

"Cast your bread upon the waters, for after many days you will find it again" (Ecclesiastes 11:1).

57

Prayer Tears

Europe

"I love prayer stories! They motivate me. They show me how others wrestle with difficulties in prayer." J. Allen Thompson, General Director of World Team at the time, wrote these words in "Pray and Praise with Us" a World Team newsletter[17]. "They encourage me," he continued, "to try new approaches in prayer." And with that Thompson related the following story:

"Please read this leaflet. It has a message for you." The young Dane held out a tract.

"Message indeed!" Why do you people bother with your religion? I'm quite capable to take care of myself." Angrily, red-haired Johannes Bach grabbed the tract, tore it in two, crumpled it in his hand and stuck it in his pocket. But as he turned to leave, he noticed the young Dane had folded his hands and bowed his head to pray. To Bach's astonishment, tears were running down his cheeks!

Back in his rooming house, Bach pulled the crumpled sheet from his pocket and began to read. Before he finished, he was on his knees asking God for forgiveness. Immediately he ran to the street, searching for the young man, but never found him. Soon after, God led him to a group of believers who rejoiced with him about what had taken place in his life.

What was the eye-opener in Bach's life? What arrested his attention on that busy street? Certainly not the outstretched arm offering a pamphlet. That made him angry. The turning point in his attitude toward God was a compassionate witness engaged in earnest prayer for him.

Bach never forgot that encounter. Years later, as a missionary and director of The Evangelical Alliance Mission, Bach prayed for every person he met. Regardless of time or place, he was always ready to pray. "He could glide from conversation to prayer—and back again—with scarcely a noticeable change of pace."

"He who goes out weeping, carrying seed to sow, will return with songs of joy, carrying sheaves with him" (Psalm 126:6).

---

[17] J. Allen Thompson, "Pray and Praise with Us," 2476 Argentia Rd., Suite 203, Mississauga, On L5N 6M1; P.O. Box 143038, Coral Gables, FL 33134; Jan. 1986.

58

Effective Short-Term Missions

Colombia

Bill Pencille (pronounced "pencil") pondered the problem of follow-up for the short-term student mission he was leading. Bill, a veteran missionary with South America Mission, was leading a group of Bible institute and college students from Canada and the U.S. that would be doing door-to-door evangelism for the next five weeks in the small town of Galapa, Colombia, ten miles from the large city of Barranquilla.

For the duration of the eight-hour bus ride to Barranquilla, Bill wrestled with the problem of providing follow-up for the people who would receive Jesus Christ as their Savior. Suddenly, he felt led to ask God to give immediate fruit almost as soon as they arrived in Galapa so that they would have the whole five weeks to disciple the new believers. In this way, they could hope to leave some spiritual work that would be more solid than that done in previous years.

The team arrived in Galapa on a Saturday afternoon. During the sharing time on the first evening, Bill talked about his burden. With great unanimity of spirit, the team wholeheartedly agreed to ask God for early results. The prayer meeting was not long or emotional, but they asked God specifically for four people whom they could disciple while they were there.

In two-and-a-half days, four young people had manifest a real interest in the gospel and had received Jesus Christ as personal Savior. True, their seeking might have been largely curiosity-based at first, but all four were also very eager to be taught in follow-up discipleship training.

The team started Bible study classes. At the end of the five weeks, Bill felt satisfied that they were leaving a more permanent work than his teams had been able to do on previous missions. Missionaries in Barranquilla were able to provide continued follow-up. Bill's next prayer was for a missionary couple to live in Galapa to build the nucleus of believers into an evangelical church.

59

Learning to Get Answers to Prayer

Alberta

"Lord, please prepare hearts for the entrance of Your Word."

"May some to whom we speak be as ripe fruit ready to be picked."

"Please help me to know what to say."

When Bible college students prepare to go to the city for door-to-door visitation, street witnessing, open air meetings on the streets or in the parks, or rescue mission services, this is what their prayers sound like. This is how it was one evening when a group went to Calgary to hand out gospel tracts and witness to people on the Eighth Avenue Mall.

As we regrouped for the bus ride back to the college, the air was charged with excitement.

"Can we take this lady over to this address?" one excited student asked the faculty advisor. "The driver says he knows where it is."

"Well, what's this all about?" asked the advisor.

"Oh, it's just wonderful to see how the Lord worked. My partner and I weren't having much success. We hadn't had any conversations to share the gospel with anyone, so we prayed together.

"When we looked up, there was this lady standing right beside us. I don't really know why I said what I did to her, but I said, 'My, you look happy.'

"And she said, 'I wish I was.'

"I could hardly believe my ears. It seemed like such a ready-made opportunity to tell her about Christ, so I said, 'Well, you can be, you know.' Then we shared the plan of salvation with her.

"When we asked whether she wanted to receive Jesus Christ as her Savior, she replied, 'Oh, yes.'

"I thought it was too easy and that she had not understood, so I went through the verses of Scripture with her again. But she still said she wanted to be saved. So we prayed with her and she asked Jesus to come into her heart right there on the street corner."

The woman had run away from her husband and children in Vancouver and was on the streets of Calgary with no money and no place to stay. The witnessing duo had called the Salvation Army and had been assured that she could stay there overnight and would be helped to return home. We took her to the Salvation Army Women's Shelter.

On the bus, we all sang, "How Great Thou Art." No one doubted that God had answered prayer.

60

Is Your Dad Saved Yet?

United States

"Years ago, I asked the Lord to preserve my mind so I could pray," remarked Mrs. Matthews. "So I won't have to worry about that. I am very forgetful, but I remember the things I pray about."

It was no surprise to Mrs. Matthews when Ron Jordahl came to Christ. Ron was a graduate assistant who taught chemistry at the University of New Mexico, and Mrs. Matthews had been praying for him for some time. She was getting along in years and her memory was poor, but she was not worried about it.

After Ron came to Christ, he shared the burden on his heart for the salvation of his father, Harry Jordahl, with Mrs. Matthews.

When Ron and his wife Faye went to see Mrs. Matthews in the State of Washington eleven years later, Ron said to Faye, "I doubt if she will remember us."

"Why, Faye! And Ron! Is your dad saved yet, Ron?" She asked the question as though she had seen them only the day before. They wondered whether her mind might be a bit confused. Seeing Ron's hesitation, she added, "Your dad's name is Harry, isn't it?" When they told her that Harry had not yet come to the Lord, she assured them that he would.

Mrs. Matthews died three years later. Her faith that Ron's dad would be saved meant a lot to the Jordahls. It was obvious that God had kept her mind for prayer and would not let those years of intercession be in vain.

Another three years passed. As Ron was serving as the librarian and faculty member at Prairie Bible Institute, he received word that his eighty-one-year-old father was dying of cancer. The family left hurriedly for Iowa as friends at Prairie prayed for Harry's salvation.

When Ron and Faye saw Harry, the transformation was evident immediately. His hospital roommate had led him to the Lord. When Harry went to be with the Lord a day later, Faye's first thought was of the meeting that would take place between the faithful prayer warrior and the man she had never met but prayed for so many years.

SECTION H

The Valley of the Shadow of Death

(Also see *Section A: Health, Healing and Suffering.*)

61

Simbas

Congo

"Burk—Dolena (McIver) Burk passed away January 11, 2001. . . . She and her husband were missionaries in the former Belgian Congo from 1945 to 1963 when her husband was killed by the Simba rebel group."

This short obituary in the *Calgary Herald* does not do justice to the exciting life that Dolena and Chester Burk lived. This is the story behind the short obituary. This is the story of two courageous people who were willing to give their lives for the gospel.

When it was nearly time for the Burks to return to their mission field, Dolena addressed a ladies' meeting. News had been coming from the Belgian Congo of killings by the Simba rebel group, and Dolena readily admitted that she was afraid to go back. (*Simba*, meaning lion, was the name the rebels had taken for themselves.) Furthermore, her doctor had warned her that she must not go back to a tropical climate because of an unusual eye condition she had. Yet, she felt that God had called them to the Belgian Congo, and he had not rescinded His call. So Dolena had prayed, "Lord, if You heal my eyes before the time for us to return, we'll know that it is Your will." Her eyes healed completely and quickly, so they went.

Several months later Dolena was back—this time without Chester. The Simbas had come at night and taken a group of people prisoner, and Chester was captured in that group. The prisoners were taken to a bridge on the Congo River where they were shot one by one. The Simbas let the bodies fall into the river to the crocodiles below.

When Dolena was rescued, she was taken in a helicopter that already had fourteen passengers in it. The helicopter had a rated capacity of seven, but it managed to land without incident.

After returning to Calgary, Alberta, just after Christmas 1963, Dolena started teaching in the Calgary school system where she stayed until her retirement in 1975.

In 1991, after twenty-eight years, Dolena made a return visit to Congo. As she descended from the plane, a large crowd broke into songs and shouts of welcome. Someone took her to her former home, and there a crowd put on a program, complete with speakers, songs and prayers. A sign, written on a bed sheet read, "Welcome to your home, Mama Burk!" Many who introduced themselves as former students from her boys' school at Boyulu said they had gone on to become pastors or church leaders.

The district conference meeting, called that same week, had to be moved outdoors under the palm trees when attendance reached 13,000. Even after her years away, Dolena had no difficulty speaking Swahili again. Her last thought as she left was that she wished she was thirty-eight instead of eighty-three.

While in Calgary, God had given Dolena an essential ministry as a prayer warrior for missions. She was a faithful and active participant in her weekly ladies' prayer meeting, and she is remembered as one who knew the importance of upholding missionaries in prayer.

Upon reading the obituary, those who knew Chester and Dolena rejoice that they are rejoicing together and with their Savior, whom they served faithfully unto death. One of these days, we can thank them for their humble, sacrificial service and rejoice with Dolena as the Lord presents Chester with the martyr's crown.

62

We Prayed, But He Died

Kansas

In the Bible college class Principles of Effective Prayer, the visiting panel members were discussing the topic, "Why Pray?" The leader posed the following questions: "When we have prayed for a sick loved one, but he dies and it seems that God has not answered our prayer for healing, what should we believe? What should be our attitude?"

Mrs. Nancy Broers, at the time a member of the home staff of Japan Evangelical Mission, replied, "God's answer sometimes is, 'No.' But whenever you pray for healing for a Christian loved one, and God takes that one Home, he or she is healed in that moment."

She gave an example, "My husband lay dying twelve years ago in Kansas City at Kansas University Medical Center. Over three hundred people were praying for his restoration. He had just gone in for minor surgery and had gotten an infection. We could not believe that it would be God's will for this man to die in the prime of life and leave behind two children, six- and seven-years-old.

"At four o'clock on a Tuesday morning, about twelve days after the first surgery, he was in God's presence. I had great peace. In spite of all those prayers? Yes, I had rest. What is better than God's good, acceptable and perfect will? We cannot improve on perfection. This is what we really want—God's highest and best, which is His will. As we pray, we must be in submission to God's will."

Pastors and other Christian counselors cannot offer comfort at such times by trying to offer reasons why God allows suffering and death. Usually, it is better just to be present, to listen, to encourage the grieving ones to cry if they feel like it, and to cry with them if the tears are genuine.

In my book *Principles of Effective Prayer*, Chapter 16, "Why Does God NOT Answer Our Prayers?"[18] examines this topic. The following paragraphs are excerpts from this book on the sub-topic, "Sovereignty of God."

> If we have met the conditions of prayer sincerely and still have not received the answer to our request, we must acknowledge God's sovereignty. The part of faith is humbly and joyfully to accept God's decision in the matter whether we understand it or not. He will give grace commensurate with the burdens He allows us to bear. All our logic may scream against it, but when God says no, or when He allows a delay in the answer, it is because His ways are not our ways nor His thoughts our thoughts. In all things God does work "for the good of those who love Him, who have been called according to His purpose" (Romans 8:28). But the greater good is "to be conformed to the likeness of His Son" (from Romans 8:29), and God alone knows what people, circumstances, suffering, disappointments and events to allow us to experience in order to bring us into conformity to the likeness of His Son.

Sometimes we can catch a glimpse of God's purposes. At other times we must walk entirely by faith.

No, we don't understand all that God is doing. Nor do we have to. Whether we walk in well-lit paths or through dark valleys, we can place our hand in His confidently.

God has a plan of the ages. Each of us fits into His design. We cannot see what the finished product will look like. It is as though we are looking on the backside of a tapestry. Someday, when we see the completed work, we will stand in awe at the marvelous wisdom of our mighty God who works all things after the counsel of His will.

Herod had James put to death by the sword. That's recorded in Acts 12:2. Peter was rescued from prison and impending death by an angel sent from God. That's only five verses later. Why was one spared and the other taken? God has not condescended to satisfy our curiosity about it. Surely the Church prayed fervently for Peter, and God answered their prayers, but should we assume that prayer was not made for James? Hardly.

When all has been said on the subject, we must come back to the fact that that there is a certain amount of mystery about requests not granted, because God has no obligation to explain His workings to us. If prayer is true, it is subjected to His will and He has the final word on the subject.

---

[18]Wentworth Pike, *Principles of Effective Prayer*, Action International Ministries CANADA;1993; 168-170.

63

Through the Valley of the Shadow

Thailand

On March 16, 1977, OMF (Overseas Missionary Fellowship) missionary Peter Wyss and his visitor Samuel Schweitzer (son of retired OMF missionaries) were ambushed and murdered about fifteen minutes from a village of the Akha tribes people in north Thailand. Their bodies were first found by Akha tribesmen, who went for police, and then by Peter's wife, Ruth, along with Joyce Parkin and Ann Burgess.

The following paragraphs are from a letter written by Mrs. Ruth Wyss on March 30, 1977, to her friends and prayer-partners. The letter was written from Switzerland after Ruth had left Thailand.

"I thought I was walking all alone
Into darkness immense and drear,
But when it was densest, a hand touched my own,
And a voice spoke gentle and clear;
'Do you not think you might have known
That I should be here?
Your need is met, your way will be shown.
Be of good cheer."   (Frank Houghton)

My Dear Friends,

A dear friend sent me this poem a few days ago, and it so aptly described my experiences that I wanted to share it with you. . . .

What still amazes me and is a great comfort to my heart is that the Lord prepared me, and the gentle and clear voice came to strengthen me even before I knew that the way would lead through immense darkness. I sensed a tremendous spiritual need on March 16. First, the Lord gave me Psalm 62 to meditate on and then in the evening, when Peter and his friend had not returned, He gave me John 14:15-18[19]. With these words, also, a deep peace came into my heart that I could only praise *Him* for all the good things *He* had put into my life.

When Joyce Parkin, Ann Burgess and I walked the trail together to ask in the Akha village why the two men had not returned, two young men told us what had happened, and later we found them along the trail. Yet, even in those darkest moments, the words sounded through my mind: "I will send you another Comforter," and I knew that *He* was right there with us, although it was still impossible to comprehend what had happened.

And from there on, during the long hours of questioning by the police, during the times I had to tell our friends, both Thai and Akha, during the funeral, *He* was there, upholding, strengthening. And praise the Lord, *He* is here now and will continue to be with my children and me in the days to come—when we will miss our Daddy so much in all sorts of ways and will find it hard to accept that he will no longer be with us. *He* will never leave us nor forsake us. . . .

So our immediate need is met, and what about the future? "Your way will be shown," says Frank Houghton in his poem. I'm sure the Lord will show the way very clearly step by step, when the time has come.

For the immediate future, I plan to work on some material for the Akha Bible School that was planned and which I hope can still be held, although Peter would have had the main lead.... So I hope to go back once more and help with the Akha Bible School. The children are with me in this.... Since we had planned on their coming out this summer, we all felt that it would be so nice if they could still make this trip. They love Thailand and so many friends there would like to see them again. Then we would all pack up and go home together. . . . I'm sure they need me now.

Thank you. . . for your prayers. We realize that in the days ahead we will so often feel homesick and long for Peter to be with us again. Pray especially that we will not give room for self-pity in our hearts. Pray that we will have courage to face life without our loving father and husband and that the thought of Peter up there with the Lord will help us to be of good cheer, knowing that we have a heavenly Father who cares.

This comes with our warmest greetings,

Ruth Wyss with
Markus, Damaris and Cornelia

God has not chosen to reveal all His purposes and goals to us now. Perhaps someday He will. But for now, it is our choice to accept His loving care and peace.

When Ruth received the request for permission to use her story, she did not remember the prayer letter at all, but gladly gave permission. She also added, "As I read the letter, my thoughts went back to that sad time, and I remember how wonderfully the Lord carried me through those first weeks and months. Many people prayed for me and my children, and I am sure that was the reason that I felt His wonderful arms underneath."

In June 1977, Ruth went back to north Thailand to help her Akha brothers with the short-term Bible School that Peter had prepared before his death. She helped the Akha brothers prepare, and they did the teaching. The people from village to village loaded them with gifts—bags, belts, beads, whatever they had.

Back home in Switzerland, after the short return to Thailand, Ruth and the children supported each other and tried to cope with their grief. Ruth, passing through the whole range of emotions that people have when they are grieving, had some very dark days and felt she could hardly face life without Peter. On some days she was angry with God for allowing Peter to be killed the way he was. She struggled, as any of us would, with rebellion and asking God why. She had doubts about God's existence, even while pouring out her grief and sorrow to Him. When the first anniversary of Peter's death came the following March, she gave up trying to be brave and just let the tears flow for days. That was the beginning of healing. She learned to take God as the father of widows and orphans. By the end of year two, she learned to say yes to the way God had led. But there were still wounds. The hardest of all was that she could not go back to her Akha brothers and sisters.

A friend had been with Peter in north Thailand with the first work party, which he had organized in 1973. At Peter's memorial service in Switzerland in 1977, God told the friend, "This is going to be your family." He turned to see who had spoken and realized that only he had heard it. Being a bachelor and enjoying his freedom, he was in no mood to acquire a family. Almost two years later, sure that it truly was God's will, Fritz Fankhauser married Ruth and her family. God has given them a joyful marriage and ministry in Switzerland and visits with the Akha in Thailand.

Fritz retired in January 2001, and together he and Ruth look forward, with their children and grandchildren, to seeing how God will bless and use them in this new experience.

[19]John 14:15-18 (KJV), "If ye love me, keep my commandments. And I will pray the Father, and he shall give you another Comforter, that he may abide with you for ever; even the Spirit of truth; whom the world cannot receive, because it seeth him not, neither knoweth him; for he dwelleth with you, and shall be in you. I will not leave you comfortless: I will come to you."

64

Dr. Matthew's Passion[20]

Uganda

When the Ebola virus hit Uganda's Gulu District, there was only one man to call for help.

(This story first appeared in the *New York Times Magazine*, February 18, 2001. By Blaine Harden.)

In the last few hours before he died, Simon Ajok seemed to explode—first in blood, then in aggravation.

The burly male nurse, who had contracted Ebola while caring for patients in an isolation ward at St. Mary's Hospital in northern Uganda, was wearing an oxygen mask when he started to hemorrhage. The oxygen had turned his blood bright red. It saturated the whites of his eyes and swelled his eyelids to near bursting. He began to bleed profusely from his nose and gums. Fighting to breathe, Simon ripped off his oxygen mask. He coughed violently, spraying a fine mist of mucous and blood onto the wall beside his bed.

Then, to the astonishment and terror of the night-shift staff in the Ebola ward, the 32-year-old nurse hauled himself out of bed. Coughing blood and muttering angrily, he lurched out of his private room and into the long hallway of the ward. Simon had pulled loose from his catheter. An IV tube dangled from his arm.

Babu Washington Stanley was a nurse on duty that night. As he would later recall, he and others on the ward retreated down the corridor while he shouted, "Please, Simon, go back!" They were covered head to toe in protective gear—rubber boots, gowns, aprons, masks, head caps and plastic eye shields. But they had never seen a critically ill Ebola patient behave like this.

Biomedical researchers admit profound ignorance about Ebola, a viral bleeding fever that first appeared in Africa in the late 1970's. There is no cure, and researchers do not know where the virus hides between human outbreaks. They do know, though, that the blood of an acutely ill Ebola patient is one of the most infectious and deadly substances on earth.

The Ebola epidemic that broke out last fall in Uganda and lasted until January was the largest ever. More than 400 people were infected; 173 died. But the patients there, even those who died, did not suffer the massive and uncontrollable bleeding from nearly every orifice that has made Ebola the dark star of the world's infectious diseases. That is, until the night Simon Ajok erupted.

"Please, Simon, go back!" Babu Washington Stanley shouted again that night, as his wildly agitated colleague stood bleeding in the hallway.

Not knowing what else to do, the nurse did what everyone at the hospital had done for years, whenever things got out of control. At 5 a.m. on November 20, he called Dr. Matthew Lukwiya.

Dr. Matthew, as he was known to his colleagues and patients, was the hospital's medical superintendent. He had helped make it one of the best medical facilities in east Africa. He was also a homegrown hero in the scrub savanna of northern Uganda.

Children playing in the dust-blown streets of Gulu, a city a few miles from St. Mary's hospital, had for years been singing a little ditty about the doctor. In it, they dared each other to jump from a high place. A broken leg would not be a problem, they sang; Dr. Matthew would fix it.

In his seventeen years at St. Mary's, a Catholic missionary hospital, much of what Dr. Matthew fixed had nothing to do with medicine. A soft-spoken, deeply religious man of forty-two, with a wide, easy smile and a slight paunch, he had stood up to a bizarre bunch of local rebels called the Lord's Resistance Army. They said they wanted to run Uganda according to the Ten Commandments. But what they had done for thirteen years was kidnap thousands of children and press them into suicidal duty as soldiers. The rebels also abducted and mutilated adults, often slicing off their lips and ears.

When rebels came to the hospital in 1989 to kidnap some Italian nuns living there, Dr. Matthew (who was an evangelical Protestant, not a Catholic) met them at the front gate and persuaded them to take him instead. He marched around in the bush for a week in his doctor's gown before the rebels let him go. He later opened the walled compound at St. Mary's as a sanctuary from the rebels. Until Ebola scared them away, about 9,000 people entered the grounds of St. Mary's every evening to sleep in peace.

The panicked call from Nurse Stanley roused Dr. Matthew from his bed. His small house was located inside the hospital compound, and the doctor made it to the Ebola isolation ward within five minutes. He suited up, as always, in boots, gown, apron, head cap, gloves and mask. He neglected, however, to put on goggles or a plastic face shield, which can protect the eyes when an Ebola patient coughs. Perhaps he was still groggy from sleep.

Simon Ajok had by then stumbled back to bed, where he was gasping for breath in his private room (one of the meager privileges afforded health-care workers who caught Ebola at St. Mary's). To help him breathe, Dr. Matthew pulled Simon, who was sticky with blood, into a sitting position. He then cleaned him up, stripping off his soaked gown and changing the soggy sheets on his bed. Simon died while the doctor was mopping the floor with bleach.

When he finished cleaning up, Dr. Matthew reviewed the events of the night with Dr. Piero Corti, an Italian missionary who, along with his wife, Dr. Lucille Teasdale, founded St. Mary's Hospital in 1961 and ran it for decades. Dr. Matthew was his chosen successor.

The more Dr. Corti listened, the more furious he became. He was exasperated by the gamble his protégé had taken.

"I wanted to strangle him," said Dr. Corti, who is 75. "I was thinking of the future and that he was the man to take care of the hospital for the next 20 or 30 years. But I didn't have the heart to tell him that. He had done what was normal for him to do."

What was normal for Dr. Matthew was a low-key combination of geniality and unyielding resolve. He flatly refused to allow anyone or anything, be it messianic rebels or bleeding fevers, to destroy his hospital. To that end, he sometimes took chances that threatened his life, such a devout Christian and such a nice guy that hardly anyone noticed his extraordinary appetite for risk.

For Dr. Matthew, the first hint of an Ebola outbreak in Uganda came on Saturday morning, October 7, when the telephone rang in his rented house in Kampala. At the time, he was temporarily living in the capital in order to finish up a master's degree in public health. After nearly a decade of running a hospital in the middle of a civil war, he and his wife, Margaret, along with their five children, decamped from the north in December 1998 and moved to Kampala.

"There seems to be a strange disease killing our student nurses," said the caller. It was Dr. Cyprian Opira, who was phoning long-distance from St. Mary's Hospital, where he was acting medical superintendent.

The strange illness, Dr. Opira said, had stumped everyone. The usual antibiotics did nothing. Stool cultures were not informative. A student nurse began bleeding from the mouth just as she died.

"We need your presence," Dr. Opira said on the phone.

Temporary escape from this kind of all-consuming responsibility had been a precious fringe benefit of Dr. Matthew's leave of absence from St. Mary's. He had taken the leave to study at Kampala's Makere University, telling his colleagues he would come back a better manager.

His wife rejoiced in the move. Kampala was 250 miles and a world away from the troubles of Gulu District and the endless responsibility of the hospital. For starters, there was no incoming artillery. At St. Mary's, a year before the move to Kampala, a mortar shell bounced off a tree and punched through the roof of Dr. Matthew's house in the hospital compound. It crashed on the floor—without exploding—not far from the bed where he and Margaret were sleeping.

War was traumatizing the children, Dr. Matthew told his wife, who couldn't have agreed with him more. The move to Kampala also gave the doctor and his wife a vacation from the demands of his being a very big man in a very poor corner of Africa.

Gulu District, which borders Sudan, is part of Acholi land, a semiarid region of goats, cows and subsistence farms long neglected by the government of President Yoweri Museveni. Electricity, for example, is turned off in Gulu on weekends, and it often goes off during the week.

In the tribal calculus that shapes politics and patronage in Uganda and across Africa, the Acholi people are viewed by Museveni's government as suspect. Museveni came to power in 1986 after waging war against an Acholi-dominated regime. During that war, Acholi soldiers murdered tens of thousands of Ugandans as part of a savage cycle of tribal killing that began in the 1970's under Idi Amin, probably Africa's most famous practitioner of brutal one-man rule. Museveni put an end to the killing and led Uganda into an era of rebuilding and relative prosperity. But Acholi land was largely left behind.

The lack of development and government services in Gulu District has been filled, in part, by successful Acholi men like Dr. Matthew. His extended family, his clan and his tribe all made constant demands on his income, his influence and his kitchen. At their home in the hospital compound, Margaret usually cooked for about twenty people at each meal; eight sat at the dining-room table, five sat in the kitchen and seven or so camped in the living room. Dr. Matthew paid school fees for the children of many of his relatives. They came to him when they were sick. And if they died, he often paid to transport their bodies back to their home villages for burial.

The move to Kampala limited the importuning of the kinfolk. Margaret remembers their twenty-two months together in the Ugandan capital as the sweetest season of their married life. Dr. Matthew loved being back in school, she said. It gave him a chance to study the latest techniques for managing the care of patients whose troubles ranged from poor hygiene to gunshot wounds to AIDS.

School had always been his salvation. He had grown up poor in the northern town of Kitgum, about an hour's drive from St. Mary's, with no strong kinship to the Acholi oligarchy in the Ugandan military. His father was a fishmonger who drowned when he was twelve. His mother was a petty trader. She fed her four sons by smuggling Ugandan tea on her bicycle across the border to Sudan, where she traded for soap. She trained Matthew to be a bicycling smuggler, but it was in the classroom where he paid close attention. He was a phenomenal student, a permanent fixture at the top of his class in grade school, secondary school, university and medical school.

With a long string of scholarships as his rope, he pulled himself up from the lowest social rung in one of Uganda's poorest regions to Acholi land.

When Matthew first showed up at St. Mary's as an intern in 1983, Dr. Corti, the Italian missionary, remembers that he and Lucille, a surgeon at the hospital, were amazed by the young doctor's intelligence and gentle ability to lead. "God sent that man here," Dr. Corti said. "Within three months of his arrival, I told my wife that he is the one who can take over. She smiled and said she was thinking the same thing. People say we groomed him to run the hospital. He groomed himself."

Dr. Matthew left Uganda for a year in 1990 to take a master's degree in tropical pediatrics at the Liverpool School of Tropical Medicine. As usual, he graduated first in his class. Dr. Bernard Brabin, who supervised his degree, said that of all the hundreds of young doctors from around the world whom he has taught in the past decade, Dr. Matthew was one of the most impressive.

"First, it was a matter of ability," Dr. Brabin said. "He

had a highly critical intelligence that adapted very quickly to complexity. He expressed himself in clear, simple ways. We encouraged him to stay in the United Kingdom, to teach and pursue higher degrees. But his commitment was the care of children in Uganda."

Unlike tens of thousands of African professionals who leave the continent for better pay and better lives abroad, Dr. Matthew apparently never even considered such a move. In letters he wrote from Liverpool to Dr. Corti at St. Mary's, he said not to worry about the hospital's future; he would be back. Even if he were to get another advanced degree, he vowed, he would come back and do his research at St. Mary's.

"Have you ever heard of a missionary temperament?" asked Dr. Brian Coulter, a senior lecturer at the Liverpool School who knew Dr. Matthew well and who visited him at St. Mary's several times in the 1990's. "That is exactly what Matthew had. His aim in life was to minister to sick children and to run one of the few institutions that function efficiently in Uganda. That is what satisfied him, and that is what he wanted."

While studying for his second master's degree in Kampala, Dr. Matthew insisted that his children take education as seriously as he did. He read to his twin nine-year-old boys every night, Margaret said, and he pestered his son, Peter, twelve, to work harder on math. For the first time in his life, he also had time to relax with his children, to follow British soccer on the BBC and to get a bit thicker around the middle.

All this came to an end, however, when the telephone rang and Dr. Matthew heard the words "strange disease." He left for the north at once, arriving at St. Mary's Hospital in the early evening, in time to witness the death of a nursing student named Daniel Ayella. As the nurse died, the whites of his eyes turned red, and blood dribbled from his mouth. Dr. Matthew had never seen anything like it.

"We thought it was something beyond our knowledge," said Dr. Yoti Zabulon, who stood beside Dr. Matthew that night and watched the nurse die. "We needed help."

The following day, a Sunday, Dr. Matthew told Sister Maria Di Santo, head of nursing at St. Mary's, that he wanted to see the charts of all patients who had died in recent weeks. He began drawing a map of suspicious deaths. It included seventeen patients, two of them student nurses. Another student nurse was also gravely ill and would soon die.

That afternoon, community leaders from Gulu District came to the hospital. They told Dr. Matthew that whole families were dying in their villages. They demanded something be done. Dr. Matthew and Sister Maria stayed up most of that night, reviewing charts and comparing symptoms with C.D.C. and World Health Organization publications on infectious fevers that caused bleeding. Their suspicion and fear, Sister Maria said, was that it was Ebola. But they had never before treated or seen patients with the disease.

What they read was based largely on what doctors had learned from the last major Ebola outbreak in Kitwit, Congo, in 1995, where 318 people got sick and four out of five of them died. The literature explained that close contact, especially unprotected exposure to an infected person's body fluids, caused most new infections. The publications also explained that the sicker a patient becomes, the more dangerously infectious he or she is. Touching dead bodies, the literature said, was a major risk.

As Dr. Matthew well knew, the dead-body factor was especially alarming in Acholi land, where tradition demands that female relatives of the deceased work together to wash and dress a corpse. After a body has been buried, those in the funeral party wash their hands together in a common basin, joined by other mourners from the village. The tradition symbolizes solidarity, but during an Ebola epidemic it was a recipe for catastrophe.

"By morning it became obvious to Dr. Matthew that it was some kind of hemorrhagic fever in our hospital," Dr. Zabulon said. "He said, 'Let's go around the usual bureaucracy and call Kampala.'"

The call was taken by Dr. Sam Okware, Uganda's commissioner of community health services, who dispatched a team to Gulu from the Uganda Virus Research Institute. When they arrived to collect blood samples, Dr. Matthew had already begun to move suspected Ebola patients into an isolation ward that he had set up following W.H.O. guidelines.

Sub-Saharan Africa is widely viewed as incapable of dealing with epidemics—for example, AIDS. In countries like South Africa and Zimbabwe, where a fifth to a quarter of the adult population is infected, AIDS will kill around half of all fifteen-year-olds, according to the United Nations. Around the world there are sixteen countries where H.I.V.-prevalence rates exceed ten percent. All sixteen are in Africa.

Uganda, however, happens to be a can-do kind of place when it comes to public health disasters. It dropped off the United Nations list of countries most affected by AIDS because its government was the first to launch a substantial awareness campaign. It distributed millions of free condoms and relentlessly explained how H.I.V. is transmitted by sexual contact. The campaign is credited with lowering the infection rate to eight percent, from fourteen percent in the early 1990's.

"Transparency, openness and modern communications, that is what we use," said Dr. Okware, the former head of Uganda's AIDS control program who was quickly named chairman of its National Ebola Task Force.

When lab tests confirmed Ebola, the Ministry of Health contacted the W.H.O., the C.D.C. and major donor nations and called a news conference. It hired more than a thousand "local informants" in 346 villages in Gulu District. They went from hut to hut, looking for sick people, who were often hidden by their families. Ebola burial teams were trained and outfitted with protective clothing. In parts of the district where the Lord's Resistance Army is active, the army dispatched armored personnel carriers to search for the sick and collect bodies. Ebola alerts filled the newspapers and the state radio.

"All dead bodies should be immediately buried in sacks made of polyethylene materials," said one typically blunt public-service announcement in a Kampala daily.

The campaign worked, but it also caused some panic. According to Dr. Okware, the rural people burned villages where Ebola was rumored to be. Officials in neighboring Tanzania and Kenya seemed to suspect that all Ugandans carried Ebola, screening them at the borders and sending hundreds home. Saudi Arabia banned Ugandans from the hajj. Even the Lord's Resistance Army blinked, releasing forty abductees it feared were infected.

Across northern Uganda, there was panic buying of Jik, a brand of household bleach manufactured in Kenya. Ebola burial teams used the stuff to soak sickbeds, douse bodies and sterilize themselves after a burial. As a result, some rural Ugandans worshipped Jik as a "miracle drug," according to Dr. Paul Onek, director of health services in Gulu District. He said they kept a bottle around the hut as a talisman to scare off Ebola. People bathed in bleach and some drank it.

"I have heard that some of you are drinking Jik to stop infection right from the stomach," Ronald Reagan Okumu, a Member of Parliament from Gulu, said at a news conference on October 30. "Nobody should drink Jik."

That same day, several hundred Acholi traditionalists took matters into their own hands in Gulu town. They tried to chase out the virus by shouting, running around with spears and beating on saucepans. They told Ugandan journalists they intended to exorcise the evil of Ebola and send it toward Kampala.

The patient load at St. Mary's soared in the week after Ebola was confirmed. By the third week of October, with the number of patients approaching sixty, the three doctors, five nurses and five nursing assistants who had volunteered to work on the isolation ward were overwhelmed.

They could not handle the load, in part, because of the time and personal attention that they gave to each Ebola patient. In other African hospitals, the treatment strategy was entirely different. Doctors encouraged a spouse or family member to be the primary caregiver for each patient. Wearing protective clothing, caregivers cooked for and cleaned up after their loved ones. The system reduced risks for nurses and nursing assistants, keeping them away from infectious body fluids.

Dr. Matthew, however, kept all kin away from infectious patients. He allowed only doctors, nurses and nursing assistants to go near them. His system helped contain the epidemic, reducing sickness and mortality rates among family members. At the same time, though, it placed health-care workers in close quarters with highly infectious patients and increased their chances of contracting Ebola. Whether it was against rebels or viruses, Dr. Matthew made a habit of taking personal risks for the sake of his hospital. In a pleasant but dogged way, he insisted that his nurses do likewise.

"There is no right answer to the question of how to nurse Ebola patients in Africa," said Dr. Daniel Bausch, a C.D.C.

medical epidemiologist who worked in northern Uganda last fall and managed the Ebola ward at a small government hospital in Gulu town. In many African hospitals, it is less a matter of best medical opinion than of what is possible. Dr. Bausch used family caregivers on the Ebola ward at Gulu hospital because he said he had no reasonable alternative. St. Mary's, though, had the facilities and the personnel to take on the care and feeding of Ebola patients without family help.

Whatever its medical or epidemiological value, Dr. Matthew's system became a management nightmare. He tried to reassure nurses and nursing assistants that the risk was tolerable. Yet as the week went by, Ebola insidiously eroded his authority. Health-care workers wore their protective gear, they managed their risks and still they got sick. Twelve of them died.

"With each death, the tension built," said Sister Maria, "You could feel the atmosphere. It was building toward a climax. There were so many questions and no answers."

To keep his volunteer nurses from bolting, Dr. Matthew tried to lead by example. He was in the Ebola ward every morning at seven and he finished up around eight in the evening. As he made his rounds, he preached caution.

"Think with your head, not with your heart," he shouted at one nurse in late October, when she rushed to clean up after a patient who had vomited on the floor. Dr. Matthew instructed the nurse to douse the vomit with bleach before going near the patient.

In the evenings after leaving the isolation ward, Dr. Matthew visited the many foreign doctors who had set up laboratories and were helping to care for patients at St. Mary's, as well as at nearby Gulu Hospital. As they ate their dinner in the compound of his hospital, he questioned them about patient care, searching for ways to keep his nurses from getting sick. Dr. Bausch, the C.D.C. medical epidemiologist who joined in these chats nearly every night for two months, said no one could give Dr. Matthew a satisfactory reason why the nurses were getting infected.

"Very few of these nurses had ever been in a situation where they had to put on gowns, gloves, masks and wash their hands after every contact with every patient," said Dr. Bausch. "Dr. Matthew was in a situation where he had no choice but to herd around inexperienced people who didn't want to be there."

The pressure on him was unending. But Dr. Bausch said that through it all Dr. Matthew was "a very kind, very mild-mannered guy who liked to make jokes," especially about the endless American presidential election. "He didn't seem as stressed as a lot of people would have been."

Privately, Dr. Matthew was afraid—for himself and for the hospital. He did not want his wife or children to come near him. On October 14, he wrote to Margaret in Kampala: "I will not be able to come to you there because we are very busy, and secondly because it would be dangerous to you, in case I am incubating the disease, although it is very unlikely. You should not also come here! The situation is very bad."

The situation in the hospital became a whole lot worse in late November. By then, the national Ebola epidemic had peaked, and the number of new cases was beginning to fall. Not so for patients and nurses inside St. Mary's.

During a twenty-four-hour period that ended at dawn on November 24, seven people died of Ebola, including three health-care workers. Two of these workers were nurses who did not work in the Ebola ward. By breakfast, news of their deaths was causing panic. If nurses who stayed away from the isolation ward could die, it seemed that anyone could die. Nurses mutinied. The day shift did not show up for work. Instead, at 8:45 a.m., about 400 health-care workers, nearly the entire staff at St. Mary's, packed into the assembly hall of the hospital's nursing school.

"We were very many and we were so scared and we were a bit aggressive somehow," said Margaret Owot, a nurse who attended the meeting and who worked on the Ebola ward. "Ebola was a disease that no one knows how it is killing, and the nurses thought everyone would die."

When Dr. Matthew heard about the meeting, he rushed to the assembly hall and demanded to know what it was that the nurses wanted.

"We are thinking that the hospital should be closed," one nurse shouted.

By this time Dr. Matthew was well versed in the art of persuading frightened health-care workers to swallow their fear. He had made a series of inspirational speeches at staff meetings and funerals. At the largest of these funerals, for an Italian nun who died of Ebola, he had spoken on November 7 of the responsibilities of love.

"It is our vocation to save life," he said then, in a talk recorded by the Reverend Matthew Odong, the vicar general of the Catholic archdiocese of Gulu and Dr. Matthew's longtime friend. "It involves risk, but then we serve with love, that is when the risk does not matter so much. When we believe our mission is to save lives, we have got to do our work."

But on the morning of the mutiny, which happened to be his birthday, Dr. Matthew apparently concluded that inspirational rhetoric would not keep the hospital open. So he used threats. "If the hospital is closed, I will leave and I will never come back to Gulu," he said, according to Dr. Owot.

He had their attention.

With the assembly hall stone silent, Dr. Matthew told the nurses, most of whom he had helped train, the story of how he had volunteered to be kidnapped by the Lord's Resistance Army. He had been afraid the rebels would kill him, but he took the risk to protect the hospital and to keep it open for patients who had no place else to go.

The kidnapping tale laid out the principles that governed his life and the circumstances under which he was willing to risk losing it. By telling the story, he challenged the nurses to live, and perhaps to die, by the values that had brought them into nursing in the first place.

If you abandon the hospital because of fear, he concluded, many patients will die, and you will be held responsible.

"For me, I felt that he gave us really a fatherly word," said Owot, a nurse who has worked at St. Mary's for sixteen years. "He made me see that if the hospital is closed and I fall sick, where would I go? Who would nurse me?"

At another long and contentious staff meeting in the same hall that afternoon, Dr. Matthew shifted back to inspiration, which was much more his style. He could not force them to stay, he said, but he would continue fighting Ebola, alone if necessary, until the virus was beaten or until he was dead.

He joined the nurses in a song. The mutiny was over.

That evening, his wife called him, and all his children came on the line to sing "Happy Birthday." But Dr. Matthew was exhausted. "Margaret, I cannot talk," he told her. "I need to rest."

A total of twenty-nine health-care workers contracted Ebola in Uganda, and seventeen of them died, according to C.D.C. Exactly how any of them got infected is not known with a high degree of certainty. But there is a consensus among doctors who worked in Uganda, as well as in Congo during previous Ebola outbreaks, about how the infection is not spread.

Simply breathing in the vicinity of people who are infected with Ebola is unlikely to make you sick. Ebola is not a "free virus" that floats around for hours in the air of an isolation ward. "There has to be a real line of transmission," Dr. Bausch said. That means direct contact with body fluids, like vomit, blood or sweat. But the experts agree that a coughing patient who is spraying mucous or blood into the air is also a threat.

"It is not known if this spray landing on bare skin is enough," said Simon Mardel, a W.H.O. consultant who often made rounds with Dr. Matthew. "It seems most likely that there has to be a break in the skin. When a patient coughs, a much more likely route of inoculation for a health-care worker is the mouth, the nose or the eyes."

Experts guess that many of the health-care workers who got sick in Uganda made a small mistake. Their protective clothing, in the equatorial heat, may have made them uncomfortable or claustrophobic. After touching a patient, they may have gotten careless and slipped a gloved finger inside their protective mask to scratch an itchy nose or rub a sweaty eye.

Almost none of the health-care workers in Uganda wore goggles at all times in the isolation wards. They quickly fogged up. As a result, a nurse couldn't find a vein for a blood sample. A doctor couldn't see a patient's face or read a chart.

"I wouldn't have my goggles on, but if I got close to a patient to listen to his lungs, I would put my goggles down," said Dr. Bausch, who makes his living by working around the world's most infectious viruses and describes himself as "incredibly careful."

During the epidemic in Uganda, complaints about foggy goggles resulted in shipments of, among other things, plastic face shields that look like upside-down hockey masks. They did not fog up like goggles, but they were far from perfect. Open at the top, they left room for particles of coughed blood to drift down into the eyes.

Like most of the doctors and nurses, Dr. Matthew did not always wear eye protection. Babu Washington Stanley, the night-shift nurse who called him out of bed on November 20, the night Ajok erupted in blood, clearly remembers that the doctor did not put on goggles or a plastic face shield that night.

Although no one can be sure, this lapse may have been what infected Dr. Matthew. In his rush to help a dying nurse whom he had helped train, he violated his own rules. He thought with his heart.

Two days after his birthday, on a Sunday Night, Dr. Matthew called his wife. She was startled by the sound of his voice. He was heavily congested and coughing.

"Margaret," he said, "I have a terrible flu."

Monday morning he had a fever. At the hospital infirmary, he told Sister Maria he had malaria. She agreed it must be malaria.

"We said malaria, but we thought Ebola," Sister Maria said.

The fever grew worse as the day went by. He canceled meetings and went home to bed. By Tuesday, antimalarial drugs had not brought down his fever. By Wednesday morning, he was vomiting, and he found it difficult to keep liquids down. Dr. Pierre Rollin from the C.D.C. ran blood tests. They were done at a lab on the hospital compound.

That night, Grace Obuu, twenty-four, who became a nurse at St. Mary's after Dr. Matthew and his wife adopted her, went to his house. He was alone, and she put him on an IV drip to help keep him hydrated. His fever was high, and he was very weak, the nurse said, but he had stopped vomiting. She was startled by the sound of his voice. He was speaking loudly and distinctly, and he was not talking to her.

"Oh, God, I think I will die in my service," he prayed. "If I die, let me be the last." Then, in a powerful voice, he sang "Onward Christian Soldiers."

Two years earlier in a Pentecostal church in Kampala, Dr. Matthew had delighted his born-again wife by raising his hand and announcing to the congregation that he, too, was born again. Always, a church-going Protestant, he had been going to church twice a week, until the "strange disease" called him away from Kampala.

The blood test came back positive for Ebola.

"When I told him, he himself asked to go to the isolation ward," Dr. Rollin said. "He said, 'Since I am the boss, I should show an example.'"

A telephone call was finally placed on Thursday afternoon to Margaret, who had heard nothing since Sunday night. Dr. Matthew had not wanted her called, saying he feared that she would take the call on her mobile phone while driving in traffic and would get in a wreck.

She was sitting on a sofa at home when the phone rang. She immediately packed her bag, hired a taxi and left for Gulu. But she was late reaching an upcountry bridge across the Nile River. Soldiers block it at night as a security measure against the Lord's Resistance Army. Margaret had to sleep in the taxi.

On Friday morning at 9:30, dressed in protective gear, including goggles, she approached her husband's bedside.

He was in Room four in the Ebola ward, next to the room where Simon Ajok died eleven days earlier. At the sight of him, Margaret began to cry, and she rushed toward his bed to hug him.

"Don't you come close to me!" Dr. Matthew warned. "You will get infected."

He called a doctor, who brought Margaret a stool. She sat about three feet away.

"You can't stay here when you are crying," he told his wife. "You will get infected. You don't have to cry. You have to be strong and pray."

She stopped crying. He asked her how the children were doing in school. He was particularly worried, he said, that Peter was not paying proper attention in math.

After about fifteen minutes, he seemed tired, and she left. That evening, he was stronger, as Margaret remembers, and his eyes were clear. He said he probably got Ebola from Simon Ajok, and he struggled to explain why he took risks that made him ill.

"Look, Margaret, it is a rough time, I know," he said. His wife recalled his words with reverent precision, as if she were reciting from Scripture. "You were not expecting this. God's will is not our will. I did not expect also to get, you know, infected. But being a person working in the foreground of this place, anything can happen. A mechanic can get his hands chopped off in a machine. Even a woman when she is cooking can get burned. So you just have to accept the situation."

Margaret became angry. "Now, I can't even touch you," she told him. "I can't even nurse you. I can't do anything. I just have to sit aside like a traitor."

"You have to accept your fate," he replied. "I don't want you to get infected. If anything happens to me, at least you will be alive to look after my children."

On Saturday, his breathing was worse. He found it difficult to speak. Ignoring his warnings, Margaret moved close enough to touch her husband through the four surgical gloves she wore on each hand. During her 20-minute visits, she held his foot.

Dr. Matthew was getting weaker by the hour, exhausting himself as he fought for breath. On Sunday afternoon his doctors asked Margaret's permission to put him on a respirator. She gave permission, but before the machine was hooked up, she went to his bedside and asked him to pray with her.

"I said, 'Be strong, fight this sickness with the blood of Jesus,'" Margaret said.

He complained that he was dry and, until the doctors shooed her away to hook up the respirator, she slipped ice cubes into his mouth with her gloved fingers.

The breathing machine seemed to be the answer. When Margaret left her husband's bedside early Monday evening, his fever had come down, the oxygen level in his blood had risen and his pulse was near normal. One doctor told her it was a miracle. Late Monday night, however, his lungs hemorrhaged. This was the worst-case scenario his doctors had feared, and they could do nothing.

Dr. Matthew died at 1:20 a.m. on December 5. By the time Margaret was notified and ran to the Ebola ward, he had been zipped up in a polyethylene bag. She asked that it be unzipped just a little so she could see his face for the last time. The corpse, she was told, was too infectious. The answer was no.

Doctors who treat Ebola are not convinced that they have a whole lot to offer any patient. They estimate that using IV drips to replace lost fluids might make a difference for about ten percent of those who get sick. For others, they guess, the seriousness of the illness depends on the genetic makeup of a patient, the amount of tainted blood or body fluid that has come in contact with a patient and the route of infection. The prick of a bloody syringe, for example, is almost certainly worse than a cough in the face.

It also depends on the strain of the virus. In Congo in 1995, about eighty percent of those infected with Ebola died. But the strain of the virus that the C.D.C. isolated in northern Uganda was different from what they found in Congo and considerably less deadly.

It was identical to a strain that caused two Ebola outbreaks in nearby southern Sudan in the late 1970's. There, in a place where medical care was all but nonexistent, the death rate was around fifty percent—roughly the same as it was last year in the best Ugandan hospitals. The numbers suggest that modern medicine, at least so far, is helpless to change the rate at which the various strains of Ebola kill human beings.

"Ebola is a tough disease," Dr. Bausch said. "I am not so sure that once someone is infected that the treatment we offer prevents more people from dying than would have died anyhow. The saddest example of that is Dr. Matthew. When he got sick, people pulled out all the stops. But it didn't matter."

Ebola is finicky, depending on who gets infected. The same viral strain, acquired in the same way on the same evening, from the same infectious patient, can kill one person, while giving another a headache. Babu Washington Stanley, the night-shift nurse, also got sick with Ebola nine days after he and Dr. Matthew struggled to care for Simon Ajok. Stanley, though, came down with the mildest case of Ebola on record in Uganda. He had a headache for a few days, and then it went away. Ebola made him hungry, he said, especially for liver. Now he is fine.

There is an amateur videotape of Dr. Matthew's burial. It is almost unbearable to watch.

According to the will he wrote in the Ebola ward in the days before his death, a grave was chosen inside the hospital compound beneath a towering banyan tree. It lay beside the grave of Lucille Teasdale, the surgeon who was the wife of Dr. Corti. Dr. Teasdale, who died of AIDS she contracted while operating on patients at St. Mary's, had been Dr. Matthew's mentor, champion and friend.

Since his body was highly infectious, he was buried the day he died. An Ebola burial team, dressed in protective gear that seemed suitable for a lunar landing, rolled up to the gravesite at 4 p.m. in a white ambulance. They whisked a simple wooden coffin out of the ambulance and lowered it into the grave with ropes. All the while, one member of the burial team sprayed the coffin, the ropes and his colleagues with Jik bleach. More a disposal procedure than a burial, it was over in less than five minutes.

On the videotape, at the moment the ambulance comes into view, the soundtrack explodes with the screaming of nurses. Earsplitting and inconsolable, in voices that fused grief, exhaustion and rage, their shrieking was the hopeless music of the funeral. The nurses were part of a crowd of several hundred people who had been warned to stay well away from the grave until it was covered with dirt.

Margaret stood at a distance with her children. She had insisted that they witness the burial. Otherwise, she believed it would be impossible for them to accept their father's death. They arrived from Kampala just thirty minutes before the service.

Many government officials, including the minister of health, had also rushed north to Gulu. During the height of the Ebola epidemic last fall, Dr. Matthew had been quoted almost daily in the Ugandan press. He had become a national icon: the fearless field commander at the center of a biological war that threatened everyone in the country. Even though the Ebola outbreak had been all but defeated by the time he died, Dr. Matthew's death rattled the country's self-confidence, suggesting somehow that the center could not hold.

For a time, the doctor's death paralyzed Uganda's fight against what was left of the Ebola epidemic. St. Mary's stopped admitting new Ebola patients. Across Gulu district, a number of health workers quit. Suspected Ebola patients refused to be taken to hospitals. According to Dr. Onek, the health officer for the Gulu District, local people were asking, "Why go to the hospital, if the big doctor has died in the hospital?"

Six weeks after the funeral, during a long and mournful conversation about the consequences of Dr. Matthew's death, Sister Maria said St. Mary's had not yet recovered, and that she doubted that it ever would. The hospital has not been able to find a new medical superintendent.

"You know, so many people relied on him," she said. "He had clear ideas about what to do with the future of the hospital. We have lost a guide. He was so clever in a way of talking to you kindly. He could lead people. That is what we have lost."

Margaret, too, felt lost. President Museveni praised her husband's courage and promised her about $2,800 as a special death benefit. But that would not be nearly enough, Margaret said, to finish building a house in Kampala or to send five children to university, as her husband had planned. She said she did not know how she would be able to honor his wishes.

The doctor who made the mistake of thinking with his heart left far more behind than a vacuum.

Epidemiologists who traveled to Gulu credit Dr. Matthew with helping to contain Ebola before it could spread. His insistence on immediately calling senior health officials in Kampala jump-started the government's public-awareness campaign. He may have saved hundreds, perhaps thousands, of lives.

As important for containing future outbreaks, C.D.C. virologists said his support for their research meant that Uganda's epidemic should produce more scientific data on Ebola than all other outbreaks in Africa combined.

"If you need it, you have it," Dr. Matthew told foreign researchers when they descended on Uganda, according to Dr. Rollin.

Access to St. Mary's laboratories allowed researchers to preserve a vast number of blood samples from Ebola patients at every stage of infection. The samples could help them to discover how Ebola triggers a cascade of immunological events that turn the bodies defenses against itself, transforming white blood cells into subversive agents that trigger the bleeding. The samples could also help them understand—and perhaps one day invent a drug to inspire—the remarkable immune response that allowed Babu Washington Stanley to shake off Ebola as if it were a mild hangover.

Father Odong, the vicar general of Gulu, said that he hoped his friend's story will offer fellow Africans a new definition of what it means to be a big man in Africa. "It is not about getting rich and having power," he said. "We should tell everyone the story of Dr. Matthew."

Whether or not his story survives, its last chapter did turn out as Dr. Matthew had hoped.

His hospital and his nation defeated Ebola, at least this time around. With no new cases in the previous twenty-one days, W.H.O. declared on February 6 that the epidemic was effectively over. The isolation ward at St. Mary's has been closed and scrubbed down and will reopen this month as a children's ward. And Dr. Matthew's solitary prayer in the week before he died was answered: among the health-care workers who fought Ebola at St. Mary's, he was the last to die.

---

[20] "Dr. Matthew's Passion," by Blaine Harden, *The New York Times Magazine*, New York City, Feb. 18, 2001; copyright by Blaine Harden and used by permission of the author.

SECTION I

Will of God and Way of Life

65

The Gift of Language

Japan

"This language is *impossible* to learn," thought Dan Bacon, until he remembered that 114 million Japanese could speak it very well. But even that profound thought did not ease his panic. Dan and Lindie had struggled with the Japanese language for a year after arriving in the country with their two small children.

"Here I am, a missionary, called by God to witness, to share Jesus Christ with the Japanese," thought Dan, "and I can hardly say, 'This is a pen,' let alone, 'God loves you and has a wonderful plan for your life.'"

He had prayed frantically that God would give him fluency. What happened? Nothing. The more he struggled in prayer, the more frustrated he became. His emotions were strained to the breaking point. He became angry and wondered, "Hey, God, are You really going to finish what You started? Whose side are You on, anyway? Are You going to help me or not?"

If he ever wanted the gift of tongues, it was then. But he did not get it. Even his superiors in the mission were beginning to suggest that maybe he needed to consider that missions wasn't his calling, at least missions in Japan.

One day he was praying and thinking, "How can I ever be a missionary if I can't speak Japanese? And if God doesn't help me, I'm not going to get it. God, You're not doing Your part!"

At that point his frustration peaked. He picked up his Bible and threw it against the wall. It flew to pieces, pages all over the place, and Dan sat down and cried like a baby.

God is good. No lightning bolt struck. The roof did not cave in. There was no earthquake. Instead, the room suddenly filled with a sense of the Presence of the Lord such as Dan had never experienced.

The Lord seemed to say, "Hey, I know how you feel. I know you hurt. I know you are frustrated. But, look, when I called you, I didn't guarantee that I would give you what you need in a moment, in an instant. I didn't say that I would bypass your normal intellect."

The realization came that God does not zap a person with a dramatic increase in I. Q. when he becomes a Christian, not even when he becomes a missionary. God works with what He has given. That takes time—a humbling thought.

Ezekiel 29:21b came to Dan's mind, "I will give thee the opening of the mouth in the midst of them; and they shall know that I am the Lord" (KJV). The Lord seemed to say to His frustrated servant, "My son, just cool it. Relax. It's all under control. I'll give you what you need."

Dan went on to have a vital part in planting three Japanese churches and became—are you ready for this?—the director of the language school! He eventually became the U. S. Director of Overseas Missionary Fellowship.

66

No Quitting!

Nigeria

"Cast your bread upon the waters, for after many days you will find it again" (Ecclesiastes 11:1).

Ecclesiastes 11:1 has been repeatedly brought home to Carol Edgar. She recently attended a church while traveling through Kano State in Nigeria, where she had once worked for eighteen years. To her surprise, the pastor knew her. He had been one of the children who had thrown stones at her as she rode past his compound on her motorcycle en route to his village of Gani many years before.

For two years Carol had visited Gani. She had gathered the young people under a big tree and had taught them to read so they could read the Bible. However, when she left, there were no known Christians. Years later, in the city of Jos, a young man, now a Bible school's acting principal, introduced himself as one of those students. He also said that five other former students are now pastors and there are many Christians at Gani.

Around 1960 Carol used to travel to the Hausa village of Barangwaje to practice her Hausa and witness for Christ. At a recent seminar in Jos for the wives of Nigerian missionaries and pastors, a woman from Barangwaje said that some of the village people had not wanted Carol to come there. To make her angry and discourage her from returning, they buried wooden spikes in the dirt path to flatten her motorcycle tires so she would have to push her bike two or three miles back to the mission station. The woman said that Carol's lack of anger at the villagers was a very powerful witness to them. There is now a very large church at Barangwaje.

67

Prayer Wishes

United States

When we walk with the Lord—maintain a constant relationship with Him, have fellowship with Him, talk everything over with Him—we make the delightful discovery that God is granting our prayer wishes. That is, instead of prayer being confined to certain times in church services, devotional periods, or times of consciously seeking the Lord it becomes continuous communion with Him, and we find that He is bringing to pass our very thoughts.

Anticipating our wishes, the Lord brings special events into our lives that we have dreamed about but never thought we would actually experience. Prayer has gone beyond words. This kind of prayer requires devotion to disciplined prayer and God's Word. It is doubtful whether anyone is aware of such communion in prayer who has not experienced it.

Elizabeth had such an experience. Having taught science and mathematics for over thirty-two years, she was thrilled to be invited to become a member of a delegation to China in 2001. She considered it, prayed about it, and, recalling Proverbs 11:14, "In the multitude of counselors there is safety," she asked her godly brother for advice. His immediate response was, "Elizabeth, you must go!"

She sent in the $500 down payment and prayed, "Father, if you want me to go to China, please provide the financial means for me to go."

Elizabeth had recently had a surgery that made it difficult for her to walk long distances or stand for long periods of time. When she shared her excitement with friends who were aware of Elizabeth's physical limitations, they began to question whether she was making a wise choice. It would be difficult, they said, for her to keep up with the group if they had long walks. Upon rereading the literature, Elizabeth learned that she would be required to carry her own luggage, something that she was unable to do because of recent surgery.

"Perhaps they are right," thought Elizabeth. "Maybe I should reconsider and find out whether they will refund my money—or at least part of it."

In contacting the organization Elizabeth learned that originally they had anticipated a group of fifteen or twenty, but 180 had signed up! They had already selected her to be a sub-leader of a group of thirty. When she mentioned her health issues, she was told that if there were times when walking was too much for her, she could sit and wait. They added that there would also be someone to carry her luggage. And, if money was a factor in her concern, she should not worry because all of her expenses had already been paid. If she canceled, they could refund only a portion of the down payment, but if she went, they would refund it all! Elizabeth realized that her first understanding of the Lord's leading must have been correct, so she proceeded with plans to go.

She noticed in the literature that some people might be able to present breakout sessions at a conference in China. She decided to prepare a discussion of how she, as a woman of faith in God, taught in a public school in the United States.

She made it a matter of earnest prayer that she might be able to weave her testimony into the speech. This was an unusual opportunity to give glory to her Lord. After many days of prayerfully preparing the talk, she submitted it to the leader of the delegation, only to have it rejected. Going into a communist country, religion would not be an acceptable topic for discussion.

Elizabeth was a bit disappointed. Again, she wondered whether she had misunderstood the Lord's directions. However, the leader of the delegation then asked her to give a presentation to the entire conference. That is, she was to address the entire group rather than a small sub-group.

Elizabeth spoke to the entire group. In response, some people talked to her about the possibility of preparing articles for publication in Chinese journals about education in the United States.

En route to China the airline had overbooked and Elizabeth got bumped for four hours. By way of apology, the airline gave her a free ticket to fly anywhere they flew in North America. In Elizabeth's first circular e-mail letter to her friends after her journey abroad, she mentioned that she had been given the ticket to "anywhere in North America."

Immediately, friends in Alberta replied by e-mail, "'Anywhere in North America!' That's our address. Why don't you come up to Alberta to visit us? We'll take you to Banff and Lake Louise and many other sites in the Canadian Rocky Mountains, and you will see some of the most beautiful country you have ever seen. We will camp in our RV and take our time visiting spectacular viewpoints of mountains, glaciers, lakes and waterfalls."

Elizabeth was amazed! Banff and Lake Louise? When she had received the free ticket, her on-the-spot question had been, "Do you fly to Banff or Lake Louise?" Upon receiving a negative reply, she said to herself, "Oh, that was a frivolous thought, anyway."

About twenty-four hours after she arrived home, she was looking longingly at a brochure with photographs of the Canadian Rocky Mountain National Parks. She prayed, "Lord, you gave me China; I can't ask for the Rocky Mountains, also." Now, within hours of her prayer, here was an invitation to the very places she had always wanted to go—and camping in an RV no less, just what she had always dreamed of. Furthermore, she would have personal guides—Christian friends from many years earlier whom she had never hoped to be able to visit.

No, that airline did not go to Calgary, the closest place to the Canadian Rocky Mountain National Parks that large planes could land. But Elizabeth used her free ticket to fly to Denver and was able to go by another airline from Denver to Calgary where her friends met her. On her way home she could visit a college friend and her husband—again, a friend she had not seen for over thirty years.

Several weeks after Elizabeth returned home from China, she went to the local grocery store. A clerk who had become a friend over the years asked what she had been doing lately. Elizabeth looked into the clerk's eyes to determine whether she really wanted to know. When urged to tell about her recent experiences, she replied, "I just returned from China, and God paid my way!"

The clerk asked to hear more and then wondered aloud in utter shock, "Do you mean that you can pray about things like that? You mean that you can pray about anything?"

Elizabeth smiled, nodded and purposed in her heart to continue the dialogue with the clerk in the near future.

68

Keep Balanced

Alberta

In 1922 it was just eight students in a little house on Canada's prairies, but now Prairie Bible Institute has all kinds of students, from kindergarteners to college and graduate students. In the last eighty years, it has become a major training resource for missionaries and Christian workers around the world. Although historically prayer has been a way of life at Prairie, there are certain prayer struggles that the late President L. E. (Leslie) Maxwell shared with me. One incident occurred in the school's third year, when the school consisted of a little group of believers Leslie jokingly called "Prairie Bible Destitute."

A leader of a large denomination negotiated with Prairie to bring it under the protective wing of his church organization. Negotiations had reached such a point that the denomination's paper carried a picture of the fledgling school as their latest addition, but actually no agreement had been consummated. Finally, in desperation, Leslie went to God for guidance: "Lord, we've got to know, we've got to know, we've simply got to know. What is to be our position? Are we to join them or not?"

He sensed the Lord telling him very clearly that this was not His direction. Not that there was any problem concerning the denomination, but God clearly negated the matter. Prairie Bible Institute remained interdenominational, although not at all anti-denominational. It has proven to be the right decision for this school, which now has students from many church backgrounds and graduates serving in numerous faith missions and denominations.

After talking about that clear-cut answer to prayer, Leslie said, "I thought after that, 'My, that's the way to get answers to prayer—God just speaking to you out of the blue every time.' But the next time I came with something of a definite, desperate character, God did not seem to answer at all! So I learned that whether it be yes, or no, the answer is good in Jesus' wonderful name."

"Keep balanced," is a saying humorously referred to as "Maxwell 1:1" at Prairie. It's a summation of Ecclesiastes 7:16-18. Verse 18 says, "The man who fears God will avoid all extremes."

Leslie practiced what he preached, and this was evident when I went to him for advice regarding Prairie's new elective course, Principles of Effective Prayer. Not one to give advice glibly, he paused in silence for a longer time than expected. Then, he said very simply, "Don't put too much emphasis on David Brainerd and Praying Hyde, those giants of the faith that prayed for days and nights on end. If you do, young housewives—mothers in your class—will say to themselves, 'Well, if that is what it takes to be a prayer warrior, count me out!'" He explained that a mother who may have sat up all night with a sick baby and then had to get breakfast and make lunches before getting her husband off to work and her children off to school would hardly be favorably impressed with stories of men who could spend days on end in prayer and fasting!

Leslie and his wife Pearl so lived the crucified life, that he taught and wrote about,[21] that they could be expected to avoid showiness or anything that might center attention on themselves rather than on the Lord.

Pearl recalled a time when one of the school's buildings burned to the ground. Sizable gifts, such as they were unaccustomed to receiving, soon came to offset the loss. The most surprising aspect was that the postmarks showed that they were sent before the fire and were on their way when it happened! "Before they call I will answer; while they are still speaking I will hear" (Isaiah 65:24).

Leslie chuckled as he remembered the time the area was desperately dry. Staff and local friends met for prayer. Afterward, the situation had changed so drastically that many of the women at the meeting had to take their shoes and stockings off to wade home!

For Leslie and Pearl, prayer was continuous fellowship with the Lord and a matter of obedience and acceptance of God's good hand. When asked about how God had answered prayer, Leslie replied, "In very insignificant ways, and yet just as real as spectacular miracles, God has answered prayer over the years—but not to satisfy our desire for the spectacular. God has to sift our motives."

---

[21]See: L.E. Maxwell, *Born Crucified* (Chicago: Moody Press 1984)

SECTION J

Christian Workers

69

An Athlete's Fall of 2,000 Feet

British Colombia

When Ron Homenuke fell 2,000 feet down the lip of a glacier, God got his attention! He uses various methods, and if it takes a near-death accident, it is better than going through life without Him.

Ron and his brothers often spent summers in their early teens with their dad in the Canadian Rocky Mountains. Dad Homenuke was a diamond driller—one who used a drill that cuts with diamonds—in the mining industry. The boys were carefree. Ron lived a life of reckless abandonment.

Ice-skating was in his blood from early childhood. He went up through the minor hockey leagues, played four years for the Calgary Centennials and then was drafted by the Vancouver Canucks on what they called "the Kid Line" because they were small. But he played with Bobby LaLonde and Rich Lemieux in Minneapolis, New York, and Philadelphia on their very first road trip.

One day a teammate's girlfriend startled Ron by saying, "Ron, I think you are an all-right guy; I'm going to pray for you, and something wonderful is going to happen to you."

One day after that, while driving his Mercury Capri with two little Pekinese pups, Bonny and Clyde, Ron stopped in Seattle to say hi to his friend Linda. When he walked into her apartment that April evening, Ron felt something. Looking back, Ron says, "The air was alive with the presence of Jesus Christ; there was an unspeakable peace and joy in the room."

Linda explained how she had accepted Jesus Christ into her heart and that peace had come as a result. As she shared with Ron, he sensed the reality, the honesty, in her words. The Holy Spirit brought a growing conviction into his heart and he accepted the Lord as his personal Savior and Lord that night. The words of Matthew 21:22 confirmed the promise of his teammate's girlfriend earlier, "And all things you ask in prayer believing you shall receive." However, Ron did not tell Linda of his inner decision.

Back home in Smithers, B.C., Ron shared his conversion experience with the only other members of his family who knew the Lord, his mother and his sister. But he still did not tell anyone else what the Lord had done for him.

For a year Ron was a silent Christian. Then in the spring, when he and his younger brother visited Christian relatives in Alberta, he began to realize his need to talk to others about the Lord. They were happy to hear of his salvation. They compared a Christian's life with a garden. If not watered regularly, it would dry up and die. They encouraged him to read the Word daily, share his joy with others, fellowship with believers and spend time in prayer.

But as Ron puts it, he "sat behind the steering wheel" of his life. Ron and Diane, a girl from his hometown, decided to get married. They didn't seek their Heavenly Father's approval, but both of them said their prayers regularly, attended church and Bible studies and had accepted Christ.

That fall Ron asked the Lord to reveal Himself to him so that he might have an intimate personal relationship with Him. He also enrolled in a Wildland Recreation course in southeastern British Columbia. Camped below the Kokanee Glacier, the first night they listened to a forest ranger's lecture. Early, the next morning, before the others were up, Ron and four friends ignored the warning sign on the cabin door and climbed to the top of the glacier.

About 9:30 a.m., after taking some pictures and sliding down snow banks, they began their descent. They had expected to slide down the snow, but the sun had made the slope icy and treacherous. They proceeded to make their way to an outcropping of rocks where they hoped to be able to climb down.

Right then, 1 Corinthians 10:12 applied to Ron all too literally; "So, if you think you are standing firm, be careful that you don't fall." Ron, in the lead with no ropes or proper hiking boots, lost his foothold and slipped over the lip of the glacier. His climbing mates thought he had fallen into a crevasse, but some of those below saw him lose his footing and tumble and slide about two thousand feet. "There I lay," Ron now reflects, "a piece of battered luggage with two skull fractures and a serious brain-stem injury."

His classmates rushed to where he lay and took turns positioning themselves beneath his body to maintain warmth while one went for the ranger. He called by radio to Nelson, B.C. for a helicopter, and Ron was in the hospital within one hour.

When Diane arrived at the intensive care unit, the nurse explained that Ron was in bad condition but living. When Diane saw him, she collapsed. She and friends waited outside the ICU for six hours, crying and wondering whether he would live.

After several days, a mercy jet flew him to Saint Paul's Hospital in Vancouver where there is a good neurological department. Three weeks after the fall, Ron regained consciousness and began a slow recovery.

Although he regained his strength, and his intelligence is good, a part of the brain was damaged. Ron would never play professional hockey again. His future looked bleak and uncertain.

When Diane told him of her plans to leave him, he couldn't blame her. She had married an up-and-coming hockey star, not a broken former athlete. But for him the wedding vows were irrevocable, and he spent many lonely nights in tears wondering what God had for him.

In 1980, Ron enrolled in Prairie Bible College. Diane sent notice and a request that he sign the divorce papers. He took the matter to the College President, Reverend Paul Maxwell. He, in turn, sought counsel from his father, President Emeritus L. E. Maxwell. They said that Ron was no longer bound to the marriage, since his wife had broken the marriage covenant and he had done all he could to be reconciled. Ron signed the papers with a broken heart.

In the summer of 1981, Ron went with an Action International Ministries (*ACTION*) Summer of Service team to the Philippines. There, God blessed him with another mountaintop experience. For the next three years, while finishing his Bible-college training, Ron coached teams of young hockey players. By the time graduation came in 1984, he had already joined *ACTION* as a full-time career missionary to the Philippines.

Damage done in the glacier fall made it very difficult for Ron to acquire the Tagalog language, but the street kids with whom he works adore him. They can communicate in English and tease him about his efforts in Tagalog. He wrestles any of them down and administers discipline with justice and mercy. To this day, Ron continues to make disciples of Filipino street kids for Jesus Christ.

70

God's Leading, God's Timing, God's Man

Korea

Thirty young Christians needed spiritual nourishment and discipleship training, and no one was available to provide it. Of the 1,300 in attendance at the Sunday morning prison service in Inchon, Korea, 130 had made a decision for Christ.

Stanley Thompson, a crewmember of Operation Mobilization's ship, the *MV Logos*, used off-duty time for evangelism and had participated in the prison service. Concerned about follow-up of those who had made decisions, he was assigned a classroom where he could meet daily to counsel thirty of the prisoners. But when the time came for the ship to sail on, who would continue to discipleship these men? Thompson was praying for someone to carry on the ministry.

Two nights before the ship was to leave, Stanley had an urge to go ashore for a walk. Up the big hill at the edge of the city he trudged, thinking and praying. At the top, he came to a statue of General Douglas MacArthur pointing back to the Philippines as he said, "I will return."

Courting couples sat on the benches around the statue, but the Christian worker found one where he could sit alone. Closing his eyes, he began praying silently, “Lord, who can go into the prison?” Security was very tight in Korea’s militant prisons. Who could possibly gain an entrance?

As Thompson prayed, someone sat down next to him. Looking up, he saw a young Korean man and heard him say something about Jesus Christ.

“Are you a Christian?” Stanley asked. Although unable to speak English, the young Korean seemed to want to communicate with him. How could Stanley communicate with him?

“Coca cola?” he asked. That is universally understood! So off they went to a little café.

Looking around, Thompson saw another young man and asked him, “Excuse me, do you speak any English?” He did and was able to explain to Thompson’s new friend that Stanley wanted him to go with him back to the ship where there was an interpreter. There, the crewman/evangelist shared his burden for someone to follow up with the prison ministry after the ship was gone.

The young Korean Christian already had access to the prison. He was already going there weekly with friends to teach a choir. Taking the names and numbers of the newly saved prisoners, the Korean Christian joyfully undertook the ministry of follow-up and agreed to continue Stanley’s efforts.

71

God's Plan From the Beginning

Mexico

Mexican Mission Ministries,[22] had prayed for an accountant for the field for a long time. This is a vital aspect of missions many Christians do not understand or think to pray about. It is not possible to be diligent in the Lord's work, meet financial obligations, and comply with government regulations without capable and well-trained people in such positions of heavy responsibility.

Twenty-five-year-old Ray Gibler from Lewiston, Idaho, studied Spanish when he was in high school to prepare for mission work in Mexico. In college he continued studying Spanish while also studying accounting. He passed three of four tests the first time to become a Certified Public Accountant and then passed the fourth on his next try. He worked for four years as an accountant and saved enough money so he could volunteer his help for eighteen months with Mexican Mission Ministries. After the time is up, if Ray feels this is the Lord's calling for him, he plans to look to the Lord to raise his support to pursue it as a lifetime career.

As the Mission's comptroller, Howard Just says, "Now, that's a plan!" Many more young people with that kind of dedication are needed on mission fields. What a joy to know that God has answered prayer for guidance and is using you to answer the prayer of others. He is the Originator, Instigator and Guide of such a plan!

---

[22]Mexican Mission Ministries, Division of Global Outreach Mission, PO Box 636, Pharr, TX 78577-0636

SECTION K

Revival

72

From War to Peace by Prayer Power

Ethiopia

(The following story, told by Dr. Bruce and Betty Adams, missionaries with SIM, Int., has been taken from the script of the SIM video by the same title.)

In southern Ethiopia—where the Wolaitta, Hadiya and Oromo tribes border each other—periodic warfare has plagued the area for centuries.

"Two years ago people from Hadiya came across the Balati River, killing many Wolaitta people, raiding houses and burning them," said Mr. Waja Kabato, President of the Wolaitta Kale Hiwot Churches.

One Wolaitta man added, "The Hadiyas came armed with rifles and machetes, but mostly with spears, strong spears."

"They stole the iron roofing sheets off the church," declared a Wolaitta lady. "Even clay pots were stolen."

"Two years ago, any person found in this place would be killed by bandits, thieves and murderers. People had to be armed with spears when they went to water their cattle. The cattle drank and were quickly driven away from the river and from danger. Committees were formed and leaders met to try to stop the conflict. Finally, they threw away the matter and gave up," said Mr. Matewos, a leader of the Hadiya Kale Hiwot Churches.

"When the warfare got serious," continued Mr. Waija, "the government sent in police to stop it. But when the police left, the raiding and plundering started again. I was greatly concerned when I heard that believers were selling their cattle to buy guns for defense and combat. In a church service, when the preacher was teaching from the Bible, if rifle shots were heard, down would go the Bible. People rushed outside, grabbed their guns and headed for the river.

"I thought to myself," Mr. Waija continued, "'Here we are sending Wolaitta missionaries to warlike tribes to preach the gospel of peace. Shouldn't the same gospel create peace here at home between us three tribes? Is our gospel dead?' Greatly disturbed by all this, I took a couple of Wolaitta church leaders to Hadiya to meet with the Hadiya church leadership. There we arranged for leaders from all three tribes to meet in Wolaitta and find a Christian solution to the problem."

Mr. Markina Maja, who was at the meeting in Wolaitta added, "We told the people, 'This killing of people is forbidden by God's Word. First, we must get down before God and repent of our sins.' We leaders knelt and confessed our sins. Also, we confessed the sin of the murderers and prayed what they should be praying."

Mr. Waja continued, "The question was raised, 'What shall we do about all the cattle and loot that was stolen?' 'Let it be lost,' was the answer. 'We will pray about the future instead of suing to get it back.' After that we said, 'What is best for the future?'"

"We decided to choose a team of five men from each tribe," said Markina. "These fifteen would meet once a month to pray that the warfare would stop. We would rotate the meeting to a different tribe's area each month. They would gather Friday evening, fasting and praying through the night, continuing until Saturday mid-afternoon. They organized other prayer groups within their own areas.

"Right after the prayer meetings started," Markina continued, "the warfare stood still. The killing stopped. Peace descended from God. Before even the next monthly prayer meeting, without us demanding, 'Give back our goods,' our enemies started bringing back the cows, bulls, calves, sheep, goats and the goods that they had stolen from us Wolaittas."

"We give thanks to God that now we all have peace," Matewos continued. "Sticks will do for driving cattle to the river. No need for spears. Even children can take the cattle to the river, and can water them. There is no danger now and no need to hurry away from the river. Hadiya and Wolaitta boys play together in the water. Women can walk alone through the desolate areas. So can children. There is even a market in the area now. People can live normally again. They have returned from the higher areas to which they fled and are able to plow in the lowlands again."

Waja agreed, "We kept on praying. After a year of no raiding or killings, we decided to hold a two-day Celebration of Peace conference right on the battlefield where blood had been spilled."

People came from Hadiya and Oromo over to Wolaitta, crossing the river, stopping for a drink or a little wash or to freshen up clothes for the meeting. Choirs came. Singers came from each of the three areas. A boy climbed a tree for a good view. His name must be Zaccheus! The crowd was challenged to send missionaries to start churches in the areas where raiding had been rampant and they vowed to keep on praying.

Ato Matewos continued, "After another nine months had passed without even one killing, we decided to hold another Celebration of Peace Conference here in Hadiya. Singers came from the three tribes. Three speakers from the three areas were thanked for their ministry and the team of fifteen prayer leaders was commended to the crowd for its support and cooperation. The three tribes, holding each other's hands up to God, joyfully sang their declaration of oneness, 'By Jesus' blood we all are one. Undivided, loving each other, hand in hand we will enter heaven.' We have sent more missionaries into areas that were previously warring. New people are accepting Christ. A new church is going up in the area."

"We praise God," added Waja, "that during the twenty-three months of peace since this prayer program began, no one has been murdered. Not even the sound of a rifle shot has been reported.

"The government is not able to maintain a permanent police force in the area. But by our prayer program, we have a force there that is permanent and continuous. We have pledged to pass this prayer tradition on to our children and to the next generations. No doubt, conflict in other situations could be stopped, if people made prayer a priority."

When asked how peace could come about and how unbelievers could voluntarily return stolen goods, Mr. Markina replies with conviction, "By prayer."

PART TWO

Personal Prayer Journeys of Wentworth and Doloris Pike

Many people have asked us to write an autobiography. Instead, we prefer to write a testimony of God's grace in our journey of prayer—not only God's gracious answers to prayer, but also the lessons He has taught us as we have prayed individually and together over the years. The Lord graciously saved us both as children, and he had us start us praying together everyday a year before we were married. We still pray together daily, and we are continuing to learn after fifty-two years of marriage.

May He receive all the glory.

73

Simon Says!

North Carolina

Simon often led in prayer in our church. Sometimes the pastor or the Sunday school superintendent called on him to pray. In the mid-week prayer meeting when anyone could pray aloud, Simon always participated.

He was a young family man, and I was a teenager. In youthful ignorance and arrogant irreverence, I made a habit of counting the number of times Simon said, "Dear Jesus," when he prayed. I smugly felt that he should know that Jesus forbade "vain repetition," and thought Simon was addressing the wrong person of the Trinity. Jesus said we should pray, "Our Father." If I felt a twinge of conscience about my critical attitude, I shrugged it off.

One Sunday morning there was a new family in church. During one of the songs before the sermon, I heard a sob. Looking up, I saw the father of the visiting family making his way to the aisle and down to the front. He knelt at the altar. No invitation had been given; the service had barely begun. It was an entirely spontaneous act. The pastor asked the congregation to be seated and pray while he counseled the man.

After a few minutes the pastor asked the visitor to tell us what God had done for him.

As nearly as I can remember, this is how he replied, "For ten years I have lived next door to Simon ________. Every week he has invited me to come to church with him, but I laughed at him and told him I didn't need his religion. Yesterday, as I was mowing my lawn, Simon and his wife were leaving to go shopping. Before getting into his car, he came over to my yard and asked me to come to church with him today. I laughed at him as usual and told him that maybe I would go to church someday—when I got old and ready to die—but I didn't need it now.

"After Simon left," he continued, "I thought about how badly I had treated my neighbor. I thought, 'In all the ten years I have known that fellow, I have not seen one thing in his life that I could point a finger at and say that he wasn't living like a Christian ought to.' The more I thought about it, the worse I felt, and the more I realized that I *do* need what Simon has.

"I could hardly sleep all night. This morning, I woke the family up and said, 'Get ready, we are going to church this morning—the church Simon goes to.' So I came here to get what Simon has. The pastor explained to me that it was Jesus I needed and told me how I could accept Him as my own Savior, so I did and Jesus has saved me."

Of course, we were all very happy that the man got saved, but to tell the truth, my happiness was mixed with a load of guilt. Simon's unsaved next-door neighbor for ten years had not found a flaw in Simon's life to criticize! Yet, here I was, a born-again Christian who had mentally mocked my brother in Christ for his habit of saying, "Dear Jesus," throughout his prayers. I quietly, but definitely, repented of my sin and promised the Lord I would never again be guilty of criticizing another person's prayers. His prayers were more effective than mine!

74

Alaska Bound Newlyweds

Nyack, New York

Doloris and I met at Nyack Missionary College in Nyack, New York. We knew that God had led us together. We had the same desire to serve Him and had both dedicated our lives wholly to Him in our teens. We also knew that God was leading us to serve Him in Alaska. I had visited her family in Louisville, Kentucky, and she had visited mine in Greensboro, North Carolina. We had the blessing of both sets of parents. It was the fall of 1949. We prayed together daily.

We planned to finish Bible college before getting married. We were corresponding with missionaries in Alaska at the El Nathan Children's Home in Valdez. They urged us to come as soon as possible, for the need there was urgent. Three years before, a fire had burned down much of the town and several buildings that belonged to the children's home. About that time, El Nathan inherited the Copper Center Road House, a hotel 100 miles inland from Valdez. This came as an unexpected and mixed blessing.

The deceased owner, who gave the road house to the children's home, had wanted the children's home to relocate to the hotel, but everyone agreed that Copper Center was too far from a port to relocate there. Richardson Highway, which led to the hotel, was only a small, dirt and gravel road and getting supplies in would have been difficult. On top of that, every spring the highway was full of frost boils (upheavals of road caused by the frost thawing). The frost boils turn into muddy holes that can become large enough to swallow whole vehicles.

About that time, a Christian friend had donated some property on Lazy Mountain near Palmer, about 255 miles from Valdez. Ken Hughes and Walter Phillips took some of the money gained from the sale of the hotel, and with a crew of teenage boys from El Nathan, went to Palmer. They cut down 500 trees and bulldozed a road two miles up the mountain to start the Lazy Mountain Children's Home. To begin with, they used surplus Quonset huts from a military base forty-eight miles away in Anchorage.

With Ken and Walter gone, it left El Nathan Home with the younger children and very little help, only Art Segerquist, his wife Louise and "Pedo" (Miss Esther Pedersen). Only two houses of the home remained since the fire, and they were about five blocks apart. "Pedo" took care of twenty to twenty-five babies and toddlers in one house with the help of a teenage girl. Art and Louise had about forty school-age children in the other. Is it any wonder that they begged us to come as soon as possible?

Back in New York state, we had begun to plan our wedding for the following summer after graduation. We also had to find some way to get missionary support. Our denomination did not work in Alaska at that time or have plans to do so in the future. And we had no contacts outside the denomination. We had no idea how the Lord was going to supply for our financial needs.

One Sunday night as we walked back to the Nyack Missionary College campus from church, we discussed Mark 11:24, "Therefore I say unto you, What things soever ye desire, when ye pray, believe that ye receive them, and ye shall have them" (KJV). We had been praying that the Lord would reveal His timing for us. But this verse seemed to be saying, "I know you want My will, but I am asking you what your will is. Because you sincerely want My will, whatever you want, just ask Me for it." Did God really mean that? Were we misunderstanding the verse? Were we influencing matters by our own desires? No, we were quite willing to wait. Furthermore, the verse said, "What things soever ye desire." We prayed together and decided to claim it. Now, the big question was, what did we really want?

Some of the more mature Christian teachers and Bible conference speakers at the school often advised students to allow a time of adjustment to married life instead of entering missionary service immediately. Therefore, we had assumed that I would seek a position as a pastor's assistant for a couple of years before going to Alaska. But what about the urgent needs of the folks at the children's home? If we should go right after graduation, wouldn't it be best to get married at the Christmas break so we would have a few months of adjustment before going right into the stressful children's home situation? Ultimately, that is what we settled on and asked the Lord for—subject to His will. We would pray and plan to be married during the Christmas holidays unless the Lord directed us otherwise.

There was one more detail. The Bible college required students who wished to get married while in school to get special permission from the proper committee. The committee often refused couples that were older than we were. The last time the committee was to meet before Christmas was on a Monday in October. During the preceding week, I wrote a letter to them but stopped short of completing it. We prayed that if it was God's will for us to proceed, He would give some clear indication where our support was to come from. Without that indication, we would not send the letter, but would follow our original plans for the next summer.

On Saturday, I returned from my weekly all-day ministry with the Bronx Messianic Center, a mission to Jews. Doloris had picked up my mail that day, and she gave it to me in the dining room at suppertime. Included in the stack was a letter from my mother.

"Dear Son," it began, "our pastor, Mr. Williams had lunch the other day with Evangelist Oliver Greene. Mr. Williams mentioned the interest you and Doloris have for missions in Alaska, and Mr. Greene said, 'Tell those young people I will stand for their financial support in Alaska.'"

I thought surely I must be dreaming. I had heard Evangelist Greene speak once, but I had never met him. And I was not aware that Pastor Williams knew of our serious interest in Alaska.

In my letter to the committee I explained how plans had developed and about my mother's timely letter. I said that we realized we were young and would gladly accept the committee's decision, whatever it was. Rather than make it a formal application, we preferred to ask their advice and follow it.

The committee debated our proposal to get married during Christmas break, and after studying my letter with the added note about my mother's letter, they granted the request. We married two days before Christmas 1949 and landed by bush plane in Valdez, Alaska, in July, 1950.

75

The Wrong Change

Cordova, Alaska

On our first trip to Alaska, we had to stay overnight in Cordova and transfer there to a bush plane. Cordova was a typical Alaskan fishing village—complete with boardwalks and false storefronts. We almost expected to see someone come around a corner wearing a holster with a six-shooter. It rained steadily. Alaska was still a U.S. territory and would not become a state for another ten years. The roadhouse, or hotel, we stayed in was a long, rustic frame building that seemed to wind around the mountain it was up against. Our room, furnished with only a plain dresser and bed, was at the end of the hall on the second floor. After depositing our luggage, we went to the little café in the next block for supper.

The clouds and rain made it dark with hardly any daylight. We were tired after our long flights from Louisville to Seattle and then on to Juneau and Cordova, so we prayed together, as we do every night, and went to bed early. We had flown over some of the most awesome glacial scenery in the world along the southeast coast of Alaska, but we were more inclined to get some sleep than to talk about it yet.

I awoke with a start. The sunshine was pouring into the window. There was not a cloud in the sky.

"Honey, wake up," I said. "We've missed our plane for sure. Our flight was for nine o'clock, but we have overslept. The sun is high in the sky."

I jumped up and hurried to the dresser for my watch. "Oh, no!" I cried. "To make matters worse, my watch has stopped. It says two o'clock." I listened, and to my surprise, it was ticking. "What does your watch have?" I asked Doloris.

Sleepily, she replied, "Two o'clock."

"Oh," I exclaimed. "We are in the Land of the Midnight Sun!" It hardly gets dark in Alaska in midsummer, but the overcast and downpour the previous evening had made me forget all about that. I went back to bed, but not to sleep.

Doloris was wide-awake by then. As I lay thinking, I asked, "How much cash did I say I had in my wallet when we got here last night?"

She told me, "You said you had only a ten dollar bill left."

"That's what I thought," I continued. "But our suppers cost only $2.50 and $3.25, so I should have $4.25 in my billfold now, but I just checked and I have a dollar more than that. I have $5.25." We thought and recounted, but there was no way to avoid the conclusion that the cashier at the café had given me a dollar too much change.

After getting a little more sleep, we made our way to the café for breakfast. It was raining as steadily as the night before. There was no evidence the sun had shone at all. I paid the cashier, then handed her another dollar and explained that the lady on duty the night before had made a mistake and had given us too much change.

"Oh, no you don't, Buster," she exclaimed gruffly. "Don't

try to pull that old one on me!"

"Lady, I don't know what you mean, but I owe you a dollar. Here it is."

"You trying to say we cheated you?"

"No, no. Please listen carefully. The cashier last night did not shortchange me—she gave me a dollar too much. So it is not my money; it's yours—or the café's—or your boss's—or somebody's—but it does not belong to me. Here, put it in your cash register."

"Now, wait a minute! You are saying we gave you too much money?"

"That's right."

"And you're giving it back!?"

"Yes, that's right."

"Well, I never!" Her hand was shaking as though I were handing her a poisonous snake when she accepted the dollar.

"You see, Ma'am, we are Christians. It would not be right to keep something that does not belong to us. I am sorry that I do not have time to explain more. We have to catch a plane right away. Here, this gospel tract will explain what it means to be a true Christian."

As we turned down the sidewalk just outside the large plate glass window, Doloris said, "Honey, look back in there." The cashier was facing the fishermen seated at the counter. Behind the row of seated men was a second row—the ones who had been eating their breakfasts in booths. They had come over to hear what the lady was saying. Holding the tract open in front of her, she pointed out the door at us and was evidently telling them the whole story.

When we had asked the Lord to help us to have opportunities to witness, this wasn't exactly what we had been thinking about. But I knew I could not have drawn such a congregation in an Alaskan fishing village on a dreary morning, no matter how hard I tried. It was one of the most attentive congregations I've ever seen before or since. It appeared that they had a good preacher too.

76

A Man Named Bible

McGrath, Alaska

The village of Sleetmute on the Kuskokwim River was about 500 air miles from Anchorage, the nearest city of any size, and about the same distance north of Bethel at the mouth of the river. By bush plane—because there were no roads across the mountains of western Alaska—you would fly 300 miles west of Anchorage to McGrath, then 200 miles down river. Any supplies, such as groceries, gasoline or roofing, had to be shipped from Seattle to Bethel and then brought upriver to Sleetmute by a stern-wheeler (paddle-wheel boat) once a year. Of course, some things could be brought in by mail plane from Anchorage, but expenses for freight were prohibitive.

Doloris and I wanted to move to Sleetmute so we could share the gospel with people who had never heard it before. We took our nine-month-old son Stephen and went as far as McGrath. There, we rented a one-room shack to stay in until we could get some basic furniture, find a house 200 miles down river (or build a log cabin) and move to Sleetmute.

By mid-summer, we realized we did not need all the things people think they need in other parts of the world. Philippians

4:19 promises, "And my God will meet all your needs according to his glorious riches in Christ Jesus." We felt our task was to determine what our needs were, and ask God for them.

It is surprising, when you think about it, how little a person really needs of this world's goods. Native families with nine or ten kids got along with only one bed per family, sometimes a table of sorts and usually no chairs at all. They sat on the bed, boxes or the floor. Wanting people to feel at ease when they visited, we decided maybe we did not need any more than anyone else in Sleetmute.

Doloris had always needed a firm mattress because of a slight deformity in a lumbar vertebra. On a half-inch sheet of plywood, mounted on four evenly cut chunks of a log, the mattress would become a good bed. Blazo boxes—empty wooden boxes that had held two cans of gasoline for Coleman stoves—were scattered all over the countryside. The boxes could serve as chairs, since we were less adept at sitting on the floor than our native neighbors were. If a box end got a crack in it so that it pinched, you could throw it out and pick up another. We already had the Coleman camp stove. In a one-room log cabin, the boxes could be nailed to the walls to become a dresser, cabinets and shelves. A straight limb could be erected on braces for a closet. I'm no carpenter, but with a few pieces of scrap lumber, I figured I could make some sort of table. So when we got right down to it, our one need was a good firm mattress.

The Northern Commercial Store in McGrath had canned groceries, rugged bush-country clothing, parkas, traps, guns, and a bit of hardware, but we had never seen any furniture there. The regular store manager, who disliked missionaries intensely, was outside on vacation. ("Outside" for Alaskans is anywhere other than Alaska.) An officer of the store, who was filling in and taking the yearly inventory, was exceptionally friendly, so I asked him about a mattress.

"Well, we have a few bed-and-mattress sets in the warehouse next door," he replied. "Let's take a look."

Just inside the door of the Quonset warehouse was a nice mahogany, drop-leaf table with upholstered dining chairs and a matching chest of drawers. As I followed the gentleman across the floor, I also saw forty Samsonite folding metal chairs.

"You interested in any of that stuff?" he asked.

"No—well, sure I am, but I don't have money to buy it," I responded honestly.

The bed-and-mattress set, with folding ends, sold for $85.

"Thanks," I said. "I'll come back when I get that much money and get one."

"Better let me quote you a price on that other stuff," the clerk remarked. "I'll give you a good price."

"Thanks anyway, but I can't afford them." I have never wanted anything in my life more than I wanted those forty chairs. There was no point in even thinking about the rest of it. But did the Lord have any place in Sleetmute for forty folding chairs?

"We'll never sell all that stuff way out here. Better let me show you what I can do for you if you aren't in a hurry. I'm taking inventory anyway."

"I have time, but I don't have even enough money for the bed."

While he calculated the price, I asked, "How in the world do you happen to have furniture like this way out here in the boonies anyway?"

"Somebody goofed. Eight years ago, when the roadhouse was built to accommodate passengers changing between the air routes and the Civil Service employees coming here, we ordered a table and chairs and a chest of drawers for each suite in the hotel. Somebody ordered one set too many."

"What about those Samsonite chairs?"

"Those were for the dance hall at the roadhouse. Beats me why forty extra!"

In calculating the amount I would owe, he subtracted shipping charges since it wasn't my mistake they were sent. Starting with the wholesale price in Seattle eight years before, he deducted ten percent for the first year, then ten percent of that and so on for eight years. The bed at $85, plus the table and chairs, chest and forty folding chairs came to $300—probably far less than the shipping alone would have cost.

I was mentally wrestling with myself: "Forty chairs for Sunday school, and Doloris would like that set, no doubt about that. But needs. We had agreed in prayer on the mattress; if the folding bed frame was thrown in, that was okay. Of course, $300 was a bargain, all right! But if we didn't have it, we didn't have it." Fact is, I had only $3.00!

I told Doloris about the bed for $85.00.

"What else?" she asked. "What are you not telling me."

Bless her, she always could read me like a book! Of course, she got it out of me.

"But we've already agreed in prayer," I reminded her. "What we need is the mattress. Since it's a set, I guess we can ask the Lord for that."

"What's the difference?" she wanted to know. "Is it any harder for God to give us $300 than it is to give us $85.00? He owns the cattle on a thousand hills, so why couldn't he just as well give us $300?"

We prayed. I agreed it would all be nice, although I didn't have a clue where we would put it all. To be honest, I don't think I prayed with much faith. But she did.

A week later a letter came from a man in Texas named Justin Bible. "Never heard of him," I said.

The letter said, "I have just heard about your work in Alaska, and the Lord laid it on my heart to send you the tithe from my $3,000 mustering-out pay from the U. S. Army." And there was the check for exactly $300! The date on it was the day I talked to the Northern Commercial man, the day Doloris started praying in faith.

77

Down the Kuskokwim

Sleetmute, Alaska

I told the man at Northern Commercial Store in McGrath how God had supplied the money for the furniture (see "A Man Named Bible") and signed the check over to him. He was amazed that someone we had never met sent the exact amount on the day he had calculated the price, especially for furniture that had been in his warehouse eight years. He assured me that we could leave it there until we found a way to ship it.

Doloris had made the acquaintance of an unsaved neighbor lady who was also astounded at the way God had answered our prayer. "But I don't know how we are going to get it 200 miles down to Sleetmute," Doloris remarked.

"Oh, I'll get my husband to take it down the river for you," the neighbor volunteered. "He has all these boats coming up the river loaded with materials, and every one of them has to go back to Bethel empty to get another load." Her husband had contracted with the government to freight all the supplies from the sea up the Kuskokwim to the radar site at Tokotna, and he had hired every available boat between Bethel and

McGrath to do it. Doloris related the conversation to me that evening.

The next morning, when I dropped by Northern Commercial, my friend behind the counter said, "I sent your stuff down to Sleetmute last night."

"What? You don't mean it has already gone! What in the world will happen to it? We don't have any place in Sleetmute to put it yet. No one there will know who owns it."

But it had gone and was probably there already. There were no telephones for hundreds of miles on the Kuskokwim. "Well," I said, "the Lord paid for it. It's His; I guess He will have to look after it."

Within a week, bush pilot Bob Vanderpool said we could rent his vacant store building in Sleetmute. We flew down river with him one evening when it would not be so hot in the bush plane.

When we landed on the grass strip behind the village at 11:00 p.m., the arctic sun was still bright. It doesn't set in late June in that part of the world. As soon as we landed everyone in the village came out, as they do when a plane arrives in Alaskan villages, day or night, summer or winter.

"Has anyone seen some furniture—a bed and a table and chairs and…."

Before I could finish, someone answered, "Must be that stuff down on beach."

Several men carried our luggage into Bob's store building, and others went down to the river's edge with me to get the furniture.

"Just showed up here one morning last week," one man said.

"Yeah, nobody know who owns it," added another. "Just woke up one morning and it was there. Nobody bother it. Think maybe some boat leave it, come back for it someday."

There it was, every piece—the table with four chairs, chest of drawers, the bed and forty folding chairs—just four or five feet from the water's edge, unharmed by weather or water and without a scratch on it.

On the following Sunday morning, the folding chairs in Bob's store building were all occupied as we presented the Bible lesson. After the service, we bowed our heads in thanksgiving for lunch and the nice furniture He had given for our little home in the wilderness. Then we dug into the black bear roast that someone in the area had given to us.

78

Storm on the Kuskokwim

Sleetmute, Alaska

After we had been in the remote native village of Sleetmute for a month, we bought a one-room log cabin with another $300 that the Lord supplied. It was over a mile from the village and most of that was water—one of the widest parts of the Kuskokwim River, which is second in size only to the Yukon.

I had no way to build a boat, so we ordered a fourteen-foot "Folbot" (foldboat) by mail from New York City. The outer shell was five ply-fabric—alternating tough rubber with layers of cord—truly tough, flexible, and virtually puncture-proof. A thin plywood framework fit snugly into the flexible shell, a narrow strip down the length for a floor, five or six ribs and two seats. It weighed about as much as an average canoe. The seats were even with the gunwales, which made the boat feel quite tipsy.

None of the natives would get in our foldboat on the river. They would have appreciated it in a calm lake for fishing or duck hunting, but there was no way you could get one of them into it on the mighty Kuskokwim. Every family had lost at least one member to drowning, and they weren't going to take unnecessary chances. When we disposed of the seats and sat on the floor plank, we felt a bit safer.

One day we were visiting Tony and Mary MacDonald at Tony's old trading post four miles down river when an Indian man came in, stood stoically for a moment, looked very sternly at me and said, "You go now!" Why was he telling me to leave? He could see that we were preparing to leave but were in no hurry, so he added, "Big storm come."

I said to Doloris, "Bring the baby, and let's go!" I had learned to trust the native peoples' weather forecast.

Pushing that little boat against the swift current of one of North America's larger rivers was a mere five horsepower outboard motor. However, we made reasonably good headway for over a mile. I determined not to follow the shoreline around a large bend in the river but to proceed in a straight line across the middle to save time. To our right, the curve of the shoreline must have been nearly a quarter of a mile away. To the left it was almost as far to a large island. The slough beyond the island was also a sizable body of water.

The head wind came up fast. At the same time, a small, but formidable black cloud moved directly toward us from over the mountain to the north, just beyond our cabin. We were still probably two miles from home. Whitecaps grew so large, they were crashing over the bow where Doloris sat holding eleven-month old Stephen. With all my strength, I held the boat steady into the north wind and against the crashing waves. I knew that if I allowed it to swerve broadside, the waves would roll us over like a toothpick. I had noticed a lone tree on the far shore to our right. After a few minutes, I looked again to see what progress we had made in relation to it. The tree was no longer there. It was ahead of us. We had been going backwards!

"Honey, pray!" I yelled.

Here, our memories differ. I thought she said, "What do you think I'm doing?" But who can trust his hearing in such wind and waves? And who can trust his memory of details in moments of panic? She was bent low over Stephen to protect him.

In a flash, we were at the muddy shore of the island! Doloris handed Stephen to me, grabbed the rope and jumped ashore. I handed the baby back to her and followed her out of the boat. She returned him to me. We pried our feet from the gumbo mud, clamored up a chest-high embankment, crawled under the willows that grew all over the island and waited. Stephen was beneath us as we sprawled on the ground. Sleet pelted us, and the willows bent so low they whipped our backs. We prayed for safety. I remembered that I had not had time to tie the boat or pull it up farther in the mud, so I prayed that it would not be driven away or battered to pieces in the storm.

Suddenly, the sleet turned to big fluffy snowflakes. The wind stopped. The willows stood upright. The black cloud was gone. The boat was right where we left it.

Without a word, we got into the little Folbot and headed home. Back in our log cabin, I said, "Honey, what happened back there?"

"I don't know," she replied. "You just turned the boat, and suddenly we were at the island."

"No," I declared, "I did not turn the boat. I was using all my strength to keep it from turning so we would not be flipped over by the waves hitting us broadside."

She said, "I don't even remember the boat going from the middle of the river to the island. We were just there all of a sudden."

"Well," I commented, "I think I remember it going to the

island, but it shot there like a bullet, and it did not rock or pitch at all. It was like hovercraft I have heard about, skimming slightly above the water. But it went as straight as an arrow."

That's it. I can't explain what happened or write a romantic ending. That is what happened, and that's all that happened. Two very grateful young parents thanked the Lord for His protection and for saving the three of us from the storm.

79

Deliverance From Tuberculosis

Sleetmute, Alaska

Mary MacDonald was dying. I knew her tuberculosis (TB) was highly contagious, but I sat up most of the night folding toilet tissues for her to spit into and put it into a coffee can for me to empty. Doloris and one-year-old Stephen were asleep in another room of the trading post.

For a while, Mary slept. Stephen started crying, so I wrapped him in his oversize parka and walked with him outside the old Alaskan trading post so he would not keep the household awake. It was minus thirty degrees Fahrenheit.

As I paced, I cried out to the Lord, "God, I'm a fool for bringing my wife and baby to this TB-riddled village. They are bound to catch it if you don't protect them supernaturally. Oh Lord, surround us by Your angels or put a shield around us to ward off the germs. I'm willing to give my life if necessary so the people can hear the gospel and some will receive Christ and be saved from an eternal hell, but God, do I have the right to endanger the lives of Doloris and little Stephen?" The tears froze on my cheeks and the night was silent. Not even a wolf-howl could be heard, let alone any voice from heaven.

I'll never forget that dreadful night of wrestling with my emotions and conscience fifty years ago. My mind raced with guilt, fear, faith, obedience and emotions, but there was no sleep and therefore no awakening from the nightmare.

Stephen seemed to be asleep again. I slipped back into the building with him and tiptoed quietly into the room to lay him beside his mother while I went back to Mary's bedside. Not much of a bed really, just a canvas army cot.

Mary, a native, had become Tony's wife when she was fourteen. Now she was thirty-four and Tony, the white trader, was seventy-four. Tony had had three other wives who had all died of TB. In the summer, a Justice of the Peace in Aniak might have legalized some marriages, but it is doubtful whether Tony ever bothered. I never asked. I just knew that it was usually too much trouble for folks to go 200 miles down the Kuskokwim just for that!

The next day, we walked on snowshoes back to our log cabin four miles up the river. In a few days, I became ill with a deep cough and congestion. Evidently the steam bath I had taken with several native men while I was at the trading post had not been a very smart idea. I went to bed, and Doloris prepared a mustard plaster for my chest and then piled the quilts and blankets on me. We were 500 miles from a doctor, with no way of getting there except to take a bush plane to McGrath, when it made the mail run, and then an airline plane to Anchorage. We didn't bother. Instead, I drank lots of hot tea and prayed. When I recovered, we figured it must have been pneumonia.

The next summer, a year after we had moved to Sleetmute, we flew to Anchorage, where Ken Hughes met us and took us to the Lazy Mountain Children's Home near Palmer. There, I would take care of the church services while Ken went on an evangelistic tour to the Aleutian Islands. While we were there, the public health nurse was giving injections to vaccinate people against TB. Doloris and Steve both got vaccinations, but the nurse wouldn't give me one, because she said I had already had TB and therefore was inoculated against it.

"No, I've never had TB," I insisted. My skin test the year before had been negative.

"Your skin test is positive," the nurse said. "You have picked it up and your body has thrown it off without your ever knowing you had it."

80

The Old Sourdough's Wife

Sleetmute, Alaska

Tony MacDonald moved to Alaska from Scotland in 1897—the early part of the gold rush. He was about twenty years old at the time, and years later he joked about how he had been so confused by the stories he had heard about Alaska that he got off the ship in Nome wearing gum boots and a fur hat! The old sourdough enjoyed spinning a good yarn.

The term *sourdough* now applies to anyone who has spent a winter in the Arctic. Originally it applied only to those who arrived in the arctic during the gold rush of 1897-98. Many of them went over the Chilkoot Pass or the Valdez glacier and had to limit their supplies severely. Each night when they bivouacked, they put a wad of the dough from biscuits or pancakes into a small jar. It soured and acted as leaven for the next batch when needed, so a supply of dry yeast was one less thing a fellow had to carry in his pack or on the sled. The name stuck to the men as surely as sourdough bread stuck to their ribs.

Tony never struck pay dirt, so he took up trapping in the

interior along the Kuskokwim River. Others partnered with him at various times, but no one lasted out a winter camping in the bush with Tony. Nick Mellick told me, "That old codger is so mean, he can't even live with himself!" Before long, Tony realized that it was more lucrative and a whole lot more comfortable to let the native folks do the trapping while he traded their furs and sold them supplies. And that's the way it was when Doloris and I, two young missionaries, met him and his wife Mary. At seventy-four years of age, Tony's trading had diminished to a few groceries he got shipped in for him and Mary and some of Mary's relatives.

Mary was thirty-four. Tony had taken her as his wife when she was fourteen. Tony had taught Mary to read and write. She had beautiful penmanship and read *National Geographic*, *Time* and *Reader's Digest*. Along with any news she got on their battery-powered radio, she kept abreast of world events better than I.

Tony's first three wives had all died from TB (tuberculosis), and Mary was dying. Tuberculosis was endangering the very existence of Alaskan native villages in the early 1950's. In Sleetmute the wry joke was often heard, "When you get TB, you get on the waiting list until you die." The only hospital for them was the Alaska Native Service Hospital in southeastern Alaska and only a small percentage of cases ever got there. No drugs for home treatment of TB existed at that time.

In the summertime Doloris and I maneuvered the four miles down river to Tony's trading post in our tiny folding boat. After freeze-up, Doloris and I walked on snowshoes, towing Stephen on his sled and carrying the .22 rifle. One of those treks took us to Mary's cot on December 31st.

Mary had heard from village folks about the Christmas

carols I was teaching. Until our arrival, they had never seen a Bible, except one written in Russian that no one there could read. It was venerated in their little tumbledown Russian Orthodox log church. Nor had they ever heard a hymn or gospel song. The carols intrigued them. Mary asked me to sing them for her.

After a few verses of "Joy to the World," and "Silent Night," I started quoting the twenty-third Psalm: "The LORD is my Shepherd, I shall not . . ." The thought crossed my mind, "Now, why am I quoting this? It is not a Christmas passage."

Tony, who had been sitting in his big overstuffed chair pretending sleep, sat bolt upright. His glasses dropped from his forehead to his nose as he thrust his index finger toward me.

"Wait a minute there, Sky Pilot" he demanded. Then, he began quoting something in a dialect I could not understand.

When he had finished, he asked in an awed tone, "Do you know what that was?"

"Sure, Tony," I replied. "I couldn't understand it, but that was Psalm 23, the Good Shepherd Psalm, wasn't it?"

"Yeah," Tony said with a far-away gaze.

"Was that highland Gaelic you were speaking?"

"Yeah. I didn't know I knew that!" he exclaimed.

"Who taught it to you, Tony, your mother?"

"Yeah."

"How old were you?"

"I don't remember. Twelve, maybe eight. I'm not sure, but I can see it now. I was standing by her knee."

Realizing that he had not been among Christians for over half a century, I was as surprised as he. I glanced at Mary and saw a look of such utter amazement as I had never seen before.

I am sure she had never heard any Scripture from the old sourdough's mouth before. She could not have guessed that he knew a word of it.

"Mary," I asked, "do you want to receive Jesus into your heart today?"

"Yes," responded Mary between her gasps for breath.

As I started to kneel beside her cot for prayer, I turned to Tony.

"Come over here and kneel with me, Tony, while Mary asks Jesus into her heart."

"Huh!" He grunted his reply as he replaced his glasses on his forehead and leaned back.

"You get up from that chair, you old codger. I don't know what you think about my Savior, and I don't care too much what you think about me, but I know how much you love this woman. I have seen how tenderly you care for her, and you have told me more than once what a good wife she has been to you. Now, you show her enough respect to get up and come over here and kneel down while we pray." And he did.

No, they did not teach me to talk like that in personal evangelism class in Bible college, but the Holy Spirit does not always lead us to use pat little formulas. I normally would not recommend speaking like that, but that's because there are not any more of the original sourdoughs around. They were a different breed and Tony knew I liked him and respected his tough, pioneering spirit.

"Do you want me to help you, Mary?" I asked.

"No." Her heavy, difficult breathing made each word very slow and laborious. She prayed without help. She told the Lord that she knew she was a sinner and was on her way to hell. She asked Him to forgive her sins and save her for Jesus' sake.

I prayed briefly, thanked the Lord for His mercy and asked Him to give her perfect assurance of her salvation. When I looked up, I saw an angel! Well, I'm not sure what an angel looks like, but that was certainly an angelic smile. Where I had seen only a dying woman, I now saw God's glory.

Three days later, on the morning of January 3, 1952, Tony walked through the big living room where Mary's cot was and saw that she was all right. He went to the kitchen to make breakfast.

"Tony!" called Mary weakly in an odd upward tone with a catch in her voice. He shuffled back as fast as his years and his bulk would permit. But Mary had left her body. She was with her Savior.

The people in the village wouldn't tell me that Mary had died. They were angry with Tony for not permitting them to have a funeral in the Russian Orthodox church. They had not had a priest in over forty years and the Eastern Orthodox rituals had become mixed up with native superstitions.

I was sick for a couple of weeks. By the time I got better, the word had leaked out about Mary, and I walked down on snowshoes to see Tony. He told me the bush pilot had strapped her body in a sitting position into the seat beside the pilot's seat in the small plane and had flown in sixty miles to the cabin where her parents were buried. The bush pilot and another man would fly up in the spring when the ground thawed and dig a grave for her.

When Tony came to the part about not allowing the villagers to "take her up to the village Russian Church and carry on over her with all that tomfoolery," he commented, "She didn't believe in all that stuff anyway. You know what she believed?"

"Yes, Tony, I know in Whom she believed, but I would like for you to tell me."

"Believed in you and your wife, that's who!" was his rejoinder.

"No, you've got it wrong there, Old Timer," I said. "She believed in our Savior."

"Have it any way you want;" he threw the words over his shoulder as he walked into the kitchen to get us some supper with some of the best bread I ever ate—sourdough biscuits.

The last I heard years ago, Tony was in the Old Sourdough Home in southeastern Alaska. I hope he trusted Jesus before he died, and that I'll see him in heaven. But I know I'll see Mary. What a glorious smile! What a joy to take the gospel to someone who has never heard it before and see that person receive Jesus into her heart!

81

Who is it, Lord?

Georgia

After a few years, Doloris and I were back “outside” (Alaskans’ term for anywhere outside Alaska) and in Georgia.

I was the pastor of a small church there, and one Sunday afternoon I was looking for a place to spend some quiet time in prayer. I knew that a Sunday school room at that time of day would be a place where I would probably not be interrupted. As I was praying, I had the impulse to pray for a certain person to come to the service that evening and receive Christ as personal Savior. I had an evangelistic message prepared, so praying for the lost was logical. However, I felt led to focus on one particular individual, I just didn’t have a clear sense of which individual.

So, I prayed for an old man in the neighborhood who I knew was hooked on cough medicine with codeine. But I had no peace about my prayer.

I tried praying about a man whose wife was a regular at church (but who came himself only on occasional Sunday evenings). He was not a believer, and I assumed he must be the one the Lord wanted me to pray for. But instead I felt the way one of my deacons had felt on one occasion when he said, "Sometimes when I pray I feel like an old wash tub has been turned upside down over my head, and my prayer doesn't go any higher than that tub!"

After several futile attempts, I decided I needed some fresh air. Perhaps I had been working too many hours, and my thinking wasn't clear. I went for a walk, but the burden would not lift. I don't think of myself as an obsessive person, but at that time I was certainly obsessed with the idea that I was to pray for a certain individual to be saved that evening. Back in the Sunday school room I said, "Lord, I don't know whether this is from You. If it is, please show me who it is I am to pray for." But He did not.

After a couple of hours, I began to realize that it was not essential that I know the person for whom I was praying. God knew, and that was all that mattered. I prayed, "Lord, I do believe that You are impressing Your will on me that I should pray for a particular individual, but I do not know who it is. I pray for the powerful convicting work of the Holy Spirit even now in the heart of the person You have in mind to come to church tonight and be saved." Peace flooded my heart, and I thanked the Lord for hearing my prayer. The burden lifted.

I shared what had happened that afternoon with the men I prayed with before each evening service. To my surprise, no one thought I was imagining things. Instead, they prayed, "Lord, please bring the person to Christ tonight—the one You laid on the pastor's heart."

Most of the folks had arrived for the service when a man and a little girl entered the sanctuary. The man looked around and stood there as though he didn't know what to do next. I had never seen him before. I walked up and introduced myself as the pastor.

"Can I join your church?" he blurted out.

"Well, let's talk about it. Maybe joining the church is not what you need right now. Maybe you need to be born again."

"I don't know what it is I need, but I've got to get right with God," he said.

"Fine, you can do that tonight." I sat down with him and showed him a few verses from Romans and from John's Gospel. Then I said, "It is time for the service to begin. After we sing a few songs, I am going to explain what it means to be born again. Why don't you have a seat and listen closely as I preach?" I did not feel that I should ask him to pray right then; he was obviously ignorant of the plan of salvation.

I preached the message that God had laid on my heart as simply and clearly as possible. The visitor seemed oblivious to anything else. I could literally see it on his face when the light dawned in his spirit. When I gave the invitation, he brought his little girl, who was about two years old, came forward and dropped to his knees at the altar. I had the joy of leading him into complete assurance of his salvation. When I asked him whether he would like to tell the congregation what the Lord had done for him, there was no hesitation.

He said, "This afternoon, about two o'clock, a strange thing happened. My wife was away visiting relatives and my little girl and I were at home alone. I was reading the Sunday comics to her when all of a sudden the strangest feeling came over me. I can't describe it, but suddenly I knew I had to get right with God. I guess I thought I was going to die. Anyway, I put the paper down and said, 'Come on, Honey, let's go for a ride.'

"I didn't know where to go for help. The only place I could think of was a little church out in the country where I went a few times as a boy. When we got there, the grass in the yard was knee high and there were boards on the windows. I didn't know what else to do or where to go, so I just sat on the steps while my little girl played in the cemetery where the grass wasn't so high. After awhile, a man came down the road, and I asked him whether there would be a service tonight."

"He said that the church had been closed for ten years, so we got back in the car and drove around. I couldn't get rid of the feeling that I had to get right with God. As I drove back into town, I came down this street. I had never driven in this part of town before. I noticed the sign in front of this church. Somehow, I just knew that this was the place I was going to find the answer. When I came in, the pastor talked to me and showed me from the Bible that what I needed was to be born again. Then, his sermon made it all so plain. I received Jesus as my Savior, and that awful feeling I had all afternoon is gone."

As our visitor spoke, I looked around at the men who had prayed with me earlier. Some of them had big grins on their faces, others had tears in their eyes, and several were saying, "Praise the Lord!" and "Amen!"

82

Too Late!

Georgia

I had just crested a small hill between Warner Robins and Macon, Georgia, when I saw that an automobile accident had occurred. The only car was upside down and a long way ahead; people were running toward it. Then I saw that quite close to me was a man lying alone in the median. I pulled off the road, and ran to him. He was on his back and blood was trickling from every orifice of his head. Beside one hand, a baby's shoes were tied together; by the other hand lay an unopened can of beer.

An Air Force officer arrived almost as soon as I did. We loosened the man's belt, and checked his collar and cuffs to avoid any obstruction to breathing. Not knowing what internal injuries were causing the bleeding, we dared not move him.

We heard a siren, and soon an ambulance arrived from Macon and stopped at the car. Attendants started loading one of the victims and covering two bodies with blankets. We could see it all, and we called as loudly as possible, but no one could hear us or see us waving frantically.

Another man appeared beside us and told us that another ambulance was on it's way from the Air Force base in Warner Robbins. After the first ambulance left, the crowd noticed us and moved our way. An Air Force officer told them to move back and give the man air.

A woman screamed, "Somebody do something. Somebody pray for him."

"I'll pray for him, but I'm afraid it is too late," said the officer. "I know this man. He was the driver and must have been thrown out when the car careened into the median. He was going to Macon to have his baby's shoes repaired. They were all drinking. I asked him less than an hour ago to receive Jesus Christ as his Savior, but he laughed at me and told me he had plenty of time. Now, I'm afraid it's too late."

He prayed. The crowd was as silent as death itself. We helped the attendants ease the man onto the gurney and into the ambulance. At the base hospital he was pronounced D.O.A. (dead on arrival).

83

A Stick of Butter

Georgia

"Dear Lord, please give us a stick of butter so the grits won't taste so flat," Doloris prayed in all simplicity and earnestness. She wasn't complaining about the grits, turnip greens and sweet potatoes we'd been eating day after day—just asking for something to improve the flavor.

We were serving a struggling little church in a small, Georgia town. We had turned three of the Sunday school rooms in the unfinished cement block building into an apartment, so we would not have to pay rent. Nevertheless, the salary did not quite cover car payments, medical bills, clothes for the two children, and food for the table. And sometimes there wasn't enough in the offering to pay the salary.

When we first accepted the call to the church, the parishioners brought groceries often but the honeymoon stage soon passed. However, one family shared several burlap bags of sweet potatoes that a farmer friend had given them. An unchurched man in the neighborhood insisted that we regularly cut turnip greens in his garden. They grew almost year-round in the mild climate. Having come from the south ourselves, we enjoy grits and feel a bit sorry for folks north of the Mason-Dixon Line who don't know what good breakfast food is. But nobody eats grits without anything to flavor them. That's why Doloris prayed for a stick of butter. She meant margarine, but we had both grown up calling it butter. I'm sure the Lord understood.

That evening someone's hard knock at our door brought us running. Fred, a friend of ours, was using the side of his foot to knock with because his arms were full of groceries.

Steaks! Chickens! Roasts! And we did not have a refrigerator.

Then I pulled out a stick of butter, not a pound, but a quarter-pound stick of margarine. "You and your great faith!" I exclaimed to my wife. "Next time, why don't you ask for a pound?"

84

Hepatitis

Georgia

Our son, four-year-old Stephen, had been sick for about three days, and we had no health insurance. It was 1954, and I had recently accepted the call to a small church in Georgia with the promise of $15.00 per week. Doloris and I owed more than that in car payments and doctor bills, but we trusted God and He was meeting every need.

We had not been able to get anything to stay in Steve's stomach since Friday—not even water—so on Sunday morning Doloris took him to the doctor. I got the Sunday school started and watched our other son, Kenn. A few hours later, Doloris brought him back with the diagnosis: Hepatitis!

Doctors did not know much about the disease at that time. We were told that there was no medication for hepatitis, and that we should just keep Steve in bed and try to give him weak broth. The doctor said he could have the hepatitis as long as nine months. By Sunday evening, Steve lay in his bed with a fever of over 105 degrees Fahrenheit. His skin and the whites of his eyes were very yellow, his eyes were half open in a glassy, unseeing stare, and his breathing was shallow and irregular.

Before the Sunday evening service several men met with me for prayer. Of course, I requested prayer for Stephen.

As Mr. Smith, a man with simple, childlike faith prayed, he cried. I suddenly had an experience that I had never had before or since. I knew that God had heard and answered. Not that He was going to heal Stephen, but that He already had. I jumped up off my knees while Brother Smith was still praying and ran down the hallway to our little three-room apartment.

I did not go to find out whether God had healed Steve. As I ran, I was rejoicing in what I knew I would see—Stephen asleep with eyes closed, breathing normal, with a normal, healthy pink skin color. When I laid my hand on his forehead there was apparently no fever. We awoke several times that night and tiptoed to his bed to reassure ourselves that he was still breathing. On Monday morning he did not want any breakfast but wanted to get up and play, which he did until noon. At lunchtime he was so hungry I thought that if Doloris did not put enough food on the table, he would eat the tablecloth and all!

Today, Steve is a pastor of a church in Manitoba. There has never been any sign since that very day in 1954 that he ever had hepatitis. Praise the Lord for His miracle-working power.

85

Hepatitis - 2nd Installment!

Georgia

In about three weeks after Stephen's instantaneous healing Doloris and I felt ill.

"Honey, I feel sick; I think I am running a slight fever," I said.

"I'm not feeling well, either," she replied.

We each took our temperatures and saw that we both had slight fevers that began to rise over the next few hours. I knew from experience that if the thermometer hit 103 degrees, I could expect delirium. My normal temperature was about 97.6 degrees instead of the usual 98.6, and when I had a fever my brain did not tolerate any 104-105 spikes. When I got to 102 degrees, I called a lady in our congregation and asked that someone come to take our boys, ages two and four, home with them since we were unable to look after them.

That telephone call was the last clear thing I remembered over the next three days. I recall trying to get out of bed only to have the floor come up and hit me in the face. Once, I was vaguely aware that a doctor was there.

When I was coherent in my thoughts, I rejoiced in the Lord, absolutely sure that He was going to heal us as he had our son. After all, I had been euphoric for about three weeks; I had seen a miracle with my own eyes. I knew what God could do. In fact, I had some thoughts of becoming a healing evangelist.

But God had other thoughts. "'For my thoughts are not your thoughts, neither are your ways my ways,' declares the LORD. 'As the heavens are higher than the earth, so are my ways higher than your ways and my thoughts than your thoughts'" (Isaiah 55:8-9). The elders of the church and another pastor, at my request, came and anointed us with oil and prayed for us according to James 5:14-16. Yet there was no improvement. Every known sin was confessed as well any sins of ignorance. We continued to get worse.

The men of the church learned that I was a veteran of World War II. I didn't mention it often because I had been too young to enlist before the fighting actually ceased. My enlistment in the US Marine Corps was about four months before the peace treaty was signed with Japan. Although legally a veteran, I felt it would be precocious to apply the term to myself. But because of my veteran status, someone realized I was entitled to admission to a Veterans Administration hospital. They picked me up, put me in the back seat of a car and drove eighty miles to the nearest VA hospital.

For three weeks, I was not allowed out of bed. Then for one week I was allowed to be somewhat ambulatory. The couple that took me home had to stop three times for me to vomit during the trip. It took a full year for me to be entirely symptom-free.

While I was in the hospital, Doloris was bed-ridden at home.

We both survived and, as this is written, have had another forty-six years to serve the Lord. "Praise the LORD. Praise the LORD, O my soul, I will praise the LORD all my life; I will sing praise to my God as long as I live" (Psalm 146:1-2).

We thank the Lord for healing our son miraculously and bringing him back from the brink of death. We thank Him also for healing us the way he did, a way that would not cause anyone to lose sight of the priority of the gospel over all physical healing.

86

The Screwball Plan

Delaware

"Please provide for my family for nine months while I complete my university degree." It was a simple and specific prayer, but I had no clue how it could be fulfilled. Our third child was on the way and that would add to normal expenses.

I had managed to make ends meet while studying at the University of Delaware by working at a secular job and preaching at a church about twenty-six miles away in Pennsylvania. But I was tired. For one year, I had worked at night in the clearance department of a large bank. Another year, I taught school five days a week and took university courses on Saturday mornings.

The Pennsylvania church was small, just a Sunday school that we were seeking to develop into a church, but it was growing and so were the responsibilities there. At this rate, it would take another three years for me to get a Bachelor of Science in Education so we could return to Alaska and teach in a remote native village.

I needed the degree so we could support ourselves while sharing the gospel in an unevangelized village. In Sleetmute, on the Kuskokwim River, the process of cutting down trees, dragging them to our one-room log cabin and sawing them up for firewood had taken as much time as the schoolteacher spent in the classroom. Plus, I often had to travel on snowshoes to visit people up and down the river. I had needed most of my time there just to exist, but with a schoolteacher's salary I could pay to have a year's supply of cordwood cut and hauled.

Not only was teaching the only means of support in the village, it would provide constant contact with the people all the time. The people came to the schoolteacher for everything: medicine, help with applications for welfare, assistance in placing orders to Sears, and completing applications to send their children away to high school.

The teacher's nightly two-way radio was the only contact with a doctor. In the 1950's a doctor got to some remote villages only once a year. Other villages from 500 to 1000 miles from the nearest road had never had a doctor's visit. The teacher had the only medicines available. The schoolteacher had a seven-day-a-week, 24-hour-a-day responsibility for all the people in the village. My Bible college diploma did not satisfy the government requirement for a teaching position, and I needed the accredited university degree in addition to my Bible/missionary training.

Scholarships galore existed for on-campus university students for room, board and tuition. However, they were not designed for a student with a family who had to pay rent, buy food and clothes, make car payments, and pay medical bills and insurance policies. By agreeing to teach in Delaware for at least a year after I received my degree, I received a Delaware State grant of $300 toward books and tuition for a summer session.

Dropping by the office of Dr. Penrose, Dean of the School

of Education, I inquired, "I don't suppose you know of any other scholarships or grants for a person in my circumstances, do you? Nothing listed in the catalog fits my need."

"Maybe I do," replied Dr. Penrose. He mentioned an unadvertised foundation that provided grants for educational needs upon the recommendation of a dean.

A few days later a simple application form arrived in the mail. There were no blanks for referrals. The Dean's recommendation, already received, was all they required. I filled in the blanks and mailed it to the foundation in Wilmington, Delaware. Within a week, a notice arrived that told me I had been awarded a $900 cash grant. I was elated.

Doloris was less exuberant. She pointed out that we could not live on $100 a month for nine months.

With typical male logic, I argued, "But, Honey, we've been managing with no help. Think what it will mean to receive another $100 a month! All I will need is a part-time job."

We had agreed that I would continue preaching at the little church, but that barely paid for our gasoline and a few groceries. When the offering was more than $15 a week, we stopped at Peter Pan on the way home and splurged on three hamburgers, one each for Doloris and me and one divided between our boys. I could not understand why she couldn't see what a blessing it would be to receive another $100 a month. She had always been so willing to sacrifice for any ministry the Lord gave us.

With her typically exasperating logic she said, "That is not what we asked the Lord for. We asked for full support so you can attend university full time.

"Well, what am I supposed to do—turn it down?" I asked.

"Ask the Lord for the rest of it, of course." How did she

get so theological? As usual, we prayed—one with faith and the other with frustration.

Several weeks passed. A postcard came asking me to call a Mr. Laird. The name sounded familiar. Yes, Dean Penrose had mentioned it. I called immediately.

"Oh, yes," responded his assistant, "May Mr. Laird have an appointment with you when you find it convenient to be in town?"

Such courtesy! My convenient time was a lot sooner than his. Two or three days later, I was in Mr. Laird's office. His job seemed to be giving money to worthy causes for one of the world's largest companies instead of paying it to the US Government in taxes. We chatted informally like old friends.

"Mr. Pike, I see that we have awarded you only $900; you obviously need considerably more than that to feed and clothe a family for nine months while you attend the University of Delaware. Now, I see," he continued, "that you also have $300 from the state for tuition and books for the summer session. According to the budget you have submitted, you need another $1400."

"Mr. Pike, do I understand that this is the minimum amount on which you can support your family?" (It was 1956. Hundreds of dollars at that time is equivalent to thousands today.)

I gulped. As I thought of the jobs that had kept me in university, I hesitated. There were ways that I could get by on less, but I would have to give account to Doloris for not sticking with what I had asked the Lord for.

"Yes, sir," I replied and started to explain that with less I could not afford hospital insurance for my family.

"Mr. Pike, we are not interested in your minimum. When we take over your educational expenses, we want you to quit working on the side and get an education. Maybe sitting in those musty university classrooms listening to boring professors is part of that. I don't know. But I don't think that's all there is to getting an education. We also want you to get some of the fringe benefits of education."

My mind was like a dog chasing its tail as I tried to make sense of what I was hearing.

"Have you ever been to a major-league baseball game?" he asked.

"Yes, sir. I did go to see the Yankee's play at Yankee Stadium one time when I was in Bible college in Nyack, New York." I wasn't sure whether I should feel guilty or not.

"Well, I think you should take your wife to see the Phillies play. It's very educational. Look, I don't know what cultural activities you enjoy—probably not the same ones I would enjoy—and I don't know very much about your two fields of interest, the ministry and education. But if you are traveling on a train someday and your seatmate can't talk about anything but baseball, I should think, if you want to talk to him about your religion, you are going to need to know something about baseball. Am I right?"

"Yes, sir."

"But maybe you would prefer the art museum—whatever is educational for you. You decide what the 'fringe benefits of education' are. Have you ever taken your children out before Christmas and painted the town red—bought them anything they wanted?"

I assured him that such a thing had never crossed my mind.

"I think you should," he laughed. "It's very educational."

Was he joking or was I dreaming?

"We call this the 'screwball plan.' It gives the auditors fits," he added, "because it's all outgo and no income. There are no strings attached. You never have to repay it. In fact, there is no way you can repay it to us. Just do what you can to help other young people who are trying to get an education whenever you can. Now if I know anything at all about your two main interests in life, you will never have much money yourself to give, but you will be in positions of influence, and you won't hesitate to ask others for help for worthy young people." He made a notation to add several hundred dollars to my budget for fringe benefits.

When our third child was born that winter, a letter came from Mr. Laird's office. "Mr. Laird is traveling in Europe," his assistant had written, "and he asked me to look after your account while he is away. Anytime we have had a new baby in our family, there have always been some unforeseen expenses. Can you use some more money?"

We could. Maternity expenses had gone up, and the car needed repairs. Soon we had another check for the amount I had indicated. On the bottom left line were the words "Screwball Plan."

The "Screwball Plan" was virtually a signed blank check from a foundation set up by a large corporation. But come to think of it, that is what all of God's prayer promises are when we fulfill the conditions of His free grace—blank checks signed by God and drawn on the bank of Heaven. Plus, it helps to have a spouse who believes in prayer and holds you to God's highest!

87

Scared of Preachers

Pennsylvania

Bruce managed a section of the University of Delaware's experimental farm. A big fellow in his early thirties, he was quite at home with large animals. However, he was scared of preachers, and he would have been the first to tell you so. He did not object to his family attending church, but he would not let his wife invite me and my family home for Sunday dinner out of fear that I would corner him about salvation. That was not my style, but I was a preacher, so he didn't trust me.

Personal evangelism techniques and appropriate Scripture verses have little effect on a man you can't talk to. But prayer can pry open the hardest heart, so we prayed.

Occasionally Bruce came to church. One Sunday evening, when I gave an invitation for anyone to come forward for prayer and to receive Jesus as their personal Savior, Bruce stepped out boldly. I asked whether he would like to receive the Lord.

"No," Bruce answered, "I already have. I came to confess Him publicly."

"Wonderful! When did this happen?" I asked.

"Thursday night. I went to an evangelistic meeting with a friend in another town. I didn't go forward when the invitation was given, but when I got home I couldn't sleep. Finally, about two o'clock in the morning, I got up and knelt by my bed and asked the Lord to save me."

88

What I Want More Than Anything

Pennsylvania

Mr. Davidson was as friendly as anyone you could ever hope to meet. He was in his sixties but not quite retirement age. I never learned his first name because he was old enough to be my father, and I was brought up to call older men "Mister."

Anytime I visited, he asked his wife to bring cake and coffee. He immediately took charge of the conversation in his gregarious manner and involved me in a discussion about the World Series or whatever his current interests were. It would take a master conversationalist to turn the talk from baseball to the things of the Lord.

When I did manage to bulldoze my way through to speak of spiritual matters, Mr. Davidson quickly acknowledged that he owed the Lord a lot.

"You know," he said, "I used to be a drunkard." He didn't use the more socially acceptable word *alcoholic*. I knew he was telling the truth because some men had told me that when they were teenagers, they had found him passed out in a ditch and had taken him home so he wouldn't freeze to death.

"But I pulled myself up by my bootstraps, as they say, and I've never touched a drop for ten years. I know God helped me a lot."

However, when I mentioned the need to be born again personally, he adroitly dodged the issue. Before I knew exactly how he did it, we were talking baseball again! It was a spiritual fencing match and he parried every thrust.

Mrs. Davidson was a sweet, genteel little lady. She was a bit shy but not too timid to ask Doloris and me to pray for her husband. She had known the Lord since her childhood, but the church she had attended had not provided much nourishment for spiritual growth. When someone invited her to our mid-week prayer meeting at The Willowdale Chapel, she readily accepted. She was so blessed by the Bible study, fellowship and prayer time that she just kept coming. Since her church had no Sunday evening service, she started coming then also.

Within two or three months she confided to a friend, "I don't get anything out of going to my church, but our family has always belonged there. We were married there, and all the children were confirmed there." In another week or two, she asked if someone could pick her up for Sunday morning services at our chapel.

Doloris and I covenanted with Mrs. Davidson to pray daily for her husband's salvation. That's how I happened to start visiting and trying to witness to him.

At first, friends from the chapel drove four miles each way to bring Mrs. Davidson to church at least three times a week. Because it was out of the way, she prevailed upon her husband's good nature to take her to church. But that meant eight miles round-trip twice for each service. Because he dropped her off and went home during each service, he was driving forty-eight miles a week!

When summer came, he decided he could sleep just as well in the car and save half the mileage. We did not have air conditioning in the little stone church, so the windows had to be open, and I can preach pretty loud when I must. When Mr. Davidson finally figured he might as well go on in since he had to listen to my preaching anyway, Doloris and I mixed a lot of thanksgiving into our prayers.

One Sunday morning, as I greeted people after the service, Mr. Davidson stood off to one side alone. When there was a break in the stream of worshipers he grasped my hand in both of his, and said quietly, "Preacher, will you say a prayer for me?"

"Why certainly, Mr. Davidson . . . ," but before I could utter another word, he had gone outdoors.

I greeted a few more families and then managed to sneak a look out the door. Mr. Davidson was standing alone on the little porch, dabbing at his eyes with his handkerchief. I saw his wife out in the yard talking to some women. Slipping out the door, I laid my hand on his shoulder.

"Mr. Davidson, you asked me to pray for you, and I will, but wouldn't you like for me to pray with you?"

"Oh, would you?"

"Sure, let's go back inside. Almost everyone has gone, and we'll find a quiet place." As we walked down the aisle, I motioned to Mr. Manley, a grand old prayer warrior in his eighties, and Paul Pyle, one of the leaders in the church, to sit near us. They did so and bowed their heads.

"Now, Mr. Davidson, you asked me to pray for you. What's on your mind? What do you want me to pray about?" I had learned not to assume too much. And I wanted him to say, "I want to receive Jesus as my Savior." But he didn't.

"The thing I want more than anything in this world is to be able to take communion with my wife," he replied.

I had preached primarily to believers that morning; it had not been an evangelistic message. Now I was perplexed as to what to make of the situation.

"Well, we served communion a few minutes ago," I declared as I silently asked for wisdom. "Didn't you take communion?" I knew the Holy Spirit was leading and that He had the situation well in hand.

"Why, no. Of course not!"

"Why not?"

"You read it yourself—right there in that Bible," he retorted a bit petulantly.

"Here is what I read," I said, as I turned again to 1 Corinthians 11 and began to read aloud, "'But let a man examine himself, and so let him eat of that bread, and drink of that cup. For he that eateth and drinketh unworthily, eateth and drinketh damnation to himself, not discerning the Lord's body'" (KJV).

"Mr. Davidson, why does that prevent you from partaking of communion?" I refused to put words into his mouth. He had parried with me long enough. I wanted to hear a clear-cut confession of his need so we could pray intelligently and specifically.

"I'm a sinner. I'm not a Christian, and I don't have any right to the Lord's table."

"What do you want to do about it?"

"I want to get saved. Isn't this how I am supposed to do it?"

"It surely is. Let's get down on our knees and talk to the Lord about it."

Someone had brought Mrs. Davidson back into the church. She sat tearfully with my wife in the back. When we arose from our knees, I motioned for them to come forward. Mr. and Mrs. Davidson fell into each others' arms and wept for joy.

"Paul, will you serve the communion, please," I asked the elder.

89

Don't Ever Speak That Name to Me Again!

Pennsylvania

Joe's wife stopped on her way out of the little chapel and asked Doloris and me to pray for her husband. Since they moved from Tennessee to Pennsylvania, he had not been going to church and was running with a pretty rough bunch from work. We made a solemn covenant with her to pray for his salvation.

Soon after that Ken, our missionary friend from Alaska, was preaching at the chapel for a week. On Sunday afternoon, he accepted my invitation to visit Joe with me.

In their living room, Joe sat in a big chair, and Ken and I sat on the couch. Joe talked about baseball. He seemed like a friendly fellow. Or he did until I asked, "Joe, do you know Jesus Christ as your Savior?"

Leaning forward in his chair and with a look of utter hatred, he shook his fist at me and said menacingly, "Don't you ever speak that name to me again; do you hear?"

A strange thing happened. The "peace that passes all understanding" flooded my spirit. Joe wasn't a particularly large man, but he was larger than I was. Ordinarily I would have had cold chills running down my back with someone's fist in my face. Yet with a calm heart and a smile, I replied, "Sure, Joe, if that's the way you want it. I will never speak to you about Jesus again—until you ask me to." His grimace changed to a startled expression as I continued without any hesitation, "Instead, I'll just talk to Him about you." With that I dropped to my knees beside the couch.

"Oh, Lord," I prayed with utmost sincerity, "what have I done? I told Joe I would never speak to him about Jesus again until he asks me to, Lord. I feel like I have this man's blood on my hands. Please, Lord, don't ever let me forget to pray for Joe even for a day, until he repents and comes to You in faith. In Jesus' name, Amen."

I don't know who had the most puzzled look, Joe or Ken, as I got up and extended my hand. "Thanks for inviting us in, Joe. I'm glad we had a chance to get acquainted." Silently he shook my hand, and Ken and I walked out to the car.

Behind the wheel my calmness evaporated, and I began to shake as I put the key into the ignition. I should not have tried to drive. "What did I do, Ken? I just told a man I would not speak to him about Jesus again!"

"Well, it surprised me too." Ken was honest. "But that is not exactly what you said. You said that you would not speak to him about Jesus again until he asks you to. I think the Lord is going to use it."

That is something I had never said to another person before, and I never intend to again. I prayed for Joe everyday. In my personal morning devotions, I prayed for Joe. At family devotions after supper, we often prayed for Joe. When Doloris and I prayed together every evening, we prayed for Joe. As I drove the twenty-six miles to the school where I taught, I often prayed for Joe. On the way home . . . well, you get the picture.

Let's fast forward to a year and a half later. I was mowing the grass in my front yard when a driver in a passing car honked his horn. I looked up, and there was Joe waving to me. He was out of sight a moment later, so I shut off the mower and ran into the house. I said to Doloris, "Honey, we have to keep praying. Joe's getting friendly; God must be working on him."

One Sunday morning, Joe came to church with his wife and children. I greeted him, and everyone was cordial to him. After that, he came several times—not every Sunday, but occasionally. Then one Sunday morning, as I walked down the aisle toward the platform, I saw Joe sitting by the center aisle without his family.

"Good morning, Joe," I said. "Glad to see you. I hope no one is sick at your house."

"No, they've just gone to Tennessee for a vacation," he replied. "I had to work, so I couldn't go with them."

As I proceeded to the platform, I was thinking, "Joe came to church and no one was at home to drag him here. Wow! Thank You, Lord."

After the service, I looked out the door and saw Joe standing in the front yard by himself smoking a cigarette. Almost everyone had gone; some were standing in little groups visiting. I went out and spoke to Joe.

He said, "Preacher, you can use my car for the vacation Bible school this week if somebody will take me to work and come and get me at five o'clock."

"Thanks, Joe. I really appreciate your offer, but the truth is that I have plenty of offers of cars, but I don't have enough people to drive them." I was thinking, "He knows that; I emphasized it from the pulpit. This is just an excuse; he really has something else on his mind."

He snuffed out the cigarette with one foot, started to say something and then quit in mid-sentence and shifted his weight from one foot to the other.

"Was there something else you wanted to say, Joe?"

"Yeah, well, I . . . No, that's okay, not really." He appeared to be quite ill at ease.

"Come off it, Joe. Something's bothering you. Do you remember that Sunday afternoon over a year and a half ago when I visited you?"

"Yeah. Yeah, I remember."

"Do you remember the promise I made to you?"

"Yeah, I remember."

"I've kept it, Joe—both parts of it. Do you know what I mean?"

"Okay, Preacher, I've had it!"

"You'll be at home alone today, won't you? Do you want me to come over?" I asked.

"Yeah. Would you do that?"

"Sure. I have a car full of youngsters that I have to take home now or their mothers will wonder what happened to them. I bring them in from the country to Sunday school and church every week. How about three o'clock this afternoon? Will that be all right?"

"Okay, I'll be there."

He sat in the same big chair. I sat exactly where I had before.

"Okay, Joe. It's your move," I stated.

When he began to talk, it was like the floodgates were opened. He talked, yes, but there were tears too. He talked for about an hour and a half. He had gone to church all his life when he lived in Tennessee. He had been the leader of his youth group and then an elder in the church. But when he moved, he started doing things with guys from his work. After that, he said his life was about "wine, women and song."

I said hardly anything—maybe an "oh" or "I see" once in awhile to let him know I was listening and interested. Finally he sobbed, and I asked, "When you were active in church work, were you born again, Joe?" I avoided saying Jesus' name for the time being.

"No."

"You understand what I mean by 'born again,' do you?"

"Yeah, I understand."

"What do you want to do about it?"

"I want to ask Jesus to save me."

I knelt in the same spot by the couch as I had a year and a half earlier. He knelt by the big chair. We prayed together, and then we hugged, cried and praised the Lord.

That was right before we moved to Canada to teach at the Prairie Bible Institute. Years later when I was visiting the chapel, I asked the pastor about Joe.

"Oh, I don't know what I would do without Joe. He's my right-hand man," he said.

I asked Joe what it was that the Lord used to bring him to Christ. He said that one Sunday morning, as the family was leaving for church and he was settling down to read the Sunday comics, his ten-year-old son asked him, "Aren't you *ever* going to take us to church again, Daddy?" And it got to him.

90

Missed It!

Pennsylvania

We had organized a little country church in Pennsylvania, but I also taught school twenty-six miles away in Delaware. I had just driven across the state line one morning when a boy about twelve-years-old came running down his driveway. I could see his school bus going on ahead. "Missed it!" I thought, so I stopped.

"Where do you go to school?" I asked. He told me and I said, "That is only a few blocks out of the way, and I have plenty of time. I'll take you there."

We got to his school faster than I expected. Before I could invite him to receive the Lord Jesus as his Savior, he said, "Thanks, Mister," and was gone.

Driving on, I prayed silently, "Lord, I sure missed it! I must have spent too much time getting acquainted. Lord, Romans 8:26-27 assures us of the Holy Spirit's intercession for us. Please follow up on that boy for me. Help him to remember what I told him." Although I forgot the boy's name the Holy Spirit brought the memory of the event to my mind often, and I prayed for him.

Twelve years after we moved to Canada, I was back at the Pennsylvania church as a visiting preacher. How things had changed! A large, beautiful structure was across the county highway from the original little stone building where I had been pastor. I was greeting people in the vestibule when a tall young man approached me with a big grin on his face. He told me his name, but it didn't ring a bell with me.

"You don't remember me do you?' he asked.

"No, I'm afraid I don't." The last name was not that of any family that had been in the neighborhood when I had lived there. Nor could I remember anyone quite that tall.

"Well, you should. You led me to the Lord," he prodded.

"What! How could I have led you to the Lord and not even remember you? Are you sure you haven't confused me with someone else?" After all, I had been away for years, and new housing developments had brought hundreds of families into the area.

"No, there is no way I will ever forget Mr. Pike. I saw in the paper that you would be speaking here this morning."

"Oh, wait a minute," I replied. "It has been twelve years since I left here. How old are you, about twenty-four or twenty-five?"

"Right on."

But that didn't help either.

"Do you remember one morning down the Wilmington Highway when a boy had missed his school bus and you...?"

"Oh! Yes, of course! No, you cannot be that boy?"

"I certainly am. I couldn't think of anything else all that day except what you had been telling me. Even in phys. ed. class that was all I could think about. When I got off the bus that afternoon, I ran down the driveway, threw my books on the kitchen table and ran upstairs to my room. I dropped to my knees by my bed and asked Jesus into my heart. I have been living for Him ever since."

Sometimes I miss it, but the Holy Spirit doesn't! He knows how to follow up.

91

Opening Soviet Nations to the Gospel

Siberia

In 1959-61, we were schoolteachers for the United States government in the little Eskimo village of Wales, Alaska. The barren coast of the Bering Strait was our front yard.

In the middle of the three-mile-wide stretch of ocean between Little Diomede Island (U.S.) and Big Diomede Island (Russian) is the International Dateline, which was also the Iron Curtain. That invisible line was as impenetrable as the Berlin Wall. The Bering Strait is only a little over fifty miles wide between the two continents; the Diomedes are pretty close to the middle. The mountains of East Cape, Siberia, were clearly visible to us from the mainland on clear days. When our family climbed one of the 1,200-1,500 foot mountains that rose steeply from the tundra behind the village, we could see far down the east coast of Asia.

I often looked at those Siberian mountains, so near and yet so unapproachable, and thought of the millions of people living across the vast expanse of land in the Soviet Union. I could hardly imagine what it must have been like to live in an atheistic country where the people were taught from infancy that there is no God, where many suffered in prison camps and some were martyred for witnessing for Jesus Christ.

I wondered why God had placed me in that position. I knew why we were in the Eskimo village, and saw that God was answering prayer and bringing many into a personal relationship with our Lord Jesus Christ. But why *that* village, that bit of sand and tundra where I could see but not visit one of the most spiritually needy empires that the world has ever known?

As soon as the question flashed across my mind, the answer came in two inaudible words: to pray. I had prayed for Russia and the other Soviet bloc nations but not regularly nor very fervently. But this was different. I prayed for the Lord to open that great land to the gospel. I told Him I would be willing to go; in fact, I said that I would like to go if I could. But I confess that I did not really expect that the monstrosity of atheism would ever be open in my lifetime. Most evangelical Christians in the West spoke of it as closed to the gospel, and I am afraid we took that for granted.

Probably the Lord had many Christians around the world praying for the people behind the Iron Curtain, people who prayed more fervently and with more faith than I. Or maybe all it takes to bring down an empire is a mustard seed.

A number of our friends from several missions are now serving in several of the former communist block nations. The Lord has never opened that opportunity to Doloris and me. He permitted me to look at the land, like Moses was permitted to see Canaan, but not to enter it. (He did permit me to take one trip to East Germany during the Iron Curtain years.) However, He gave us the greatest ministry of all: intercessory prayer.

During our devotional times together, Doloris and I pray for a missionary couple in the former most officially atheistic country in the world, Albania. It was allied with Russia until 1961, when it broke with Russia and allied itself with China. Shirley, a student who used to grade Bible college papers for me, is a missionary there now with her husband Geoff. I had prayed for Albania many times over the years, so why was I so surprised when God sent a former student grader there with the gospel?

We pray for our personal friends in Siberia, Kazakhstan and Yugoslavia. In some of the former Soviet Republics, competing religions are now bigger opponents of the gospel than communism. Isn't God, who brought down the blasphemous superpower, able to bring down the atheistic governments of China, Cuba and the terrorist Muslim powers so that the gospel might be proclaimed freely?

92

What's the Next Step?

Wales, Alaska

Teaching in an Eskimo village on the beach of the Bering Strait in Alaska had its advantages. Obviously, because of the U.S. separation of church and state, we were not allowed to turn a teacher's desk into a pulpit or an altar. However, we did manage to witness for Christ.

When questioned by the government superintendent in our orientation in Juneau, I pointed out that our salary was represented to Congress on the basis of a forty-hour week. We intended to live and witness for Christ wherever we lived. In the hours beyond the forty-hour work week, it was our business, not that of the U.S. Government or any of its agencies, whether we witnessed for Christ personally, preached occasionally in the local church, taught Sunday school or had a Good News Club in our living quarters on Sunday afternoons. (I had delved into the pertinent issues pretty thoroughly while in the university and felt confident in my position.)

After mulling that over for a few moments, to my surprise the superintendent extended has hand and said, "Mr. Pike, I think we understand each other."

During our two year tour of duty in the village, we had seen God work as we opened our home to missionaries. The Lord permitted us financially to help missionaries fly into the village to hold special evangelistic services. Souls had come to Christ and whole families had been changed for His glory.

However, the time had come when we realized that God was going to have us move on. Doloris was expecting our fourth child. When the new baby arrived, we wanted her to give her full attention to the children and not teach school.

When I told the government supervisor in Nome that Doloris had lost seventeen pounds during her first four months of pregnancy, his immediate reply by radio-telephone was, "Get her out of there as soon as possible." A tiny village, 150 miles by air from a doctor and about 900 air miles from an adequate hospital was not the best scenario for a pregnant schoolteacher whose prognosis left some doubts. He did not want the responsibility.

Doloris was going to have to fly outside Alaska with our third son Gordon, and I would have to keep the two older boys.

The big question was: What next? Where would we go, and what would we do after the baby arrived? We were glad we had an established daily prayer time together. At such times, it is good to be on comfortable talking terms with the Lord!

Late on a Saturday morning in January, Doloris and I sat at the breakfast table. The boys had gone outdoors to play. As we talked and prayed, I remarked, "You know, I have been thinking about the possibility of going back to Prairie Bible Institute." I had taught at Prairie's Christian grade school in Alberta, Canada, for one year while waiting for the appointment in Alaska.

To my surprise, Doloris replied, "So have I, but I am not sure."

"Well, why don't I write and inquire about their needs?" I asked.

"No, I would rather you didn't. If they wrote to us and asked us to come, I would know it was God's will."

"Honey, they are not going to do that," I argued. "They know we only went there for one year until we could get our teaching assignment in a village in Alaska. And besides, I don't think they write to people out of the blue asking them to join the staff. The administrators there spend time in prayer seeking God's will and asking Him to send the right personnel."

"Well, that's all the more reason that I would know it is God's will if they ask us," was her reasoning—which has always escaped my logic! So we prayed, but it seemed like "putting out the fleece" to me, and theologically, I knew that was for people of weak faith like Gideon, not for people who had the completed written Word to stand on by faith.

About that time the mail plane flew over. Because of bad weather, it was the first mail delivery since before Christmas three weeks earlier.

After mail call, I came back into our apartment with both arms loaded. There were children's magazines for the school, government bulletins and catalogs. In the whole stack of mail that I dumped on the living room couch, one airmail envelope seemed to demand my attention. In the upper-left corner was the return address: Prairie Bible Institute, Three Hills, Alberta, CANADA.

"Honey," I said to Doloris," I have a strange feeling about this letter. Why would Prairie be writing to us?"

When I opened it, I pulled out a receipt for subscriptions

to the Young Pilot magazine that I had ordered for Christmas presents for our nieces and nephews. "Oh, that's all it is," I sighed as I pulled the sheet of stationery out also.

"Dear Brother Pike," wrote Mr. Muddle, the Personnel Director. "Would you consider coming back to teach at Prairie in the fall?" I could scarcely believe it. I couldn't read it aloud to Doloris without my voice quivering and cracking, so I handed it to her.

Within ten minutes, before examining the rest of the mail, I was at the typewriter.

"Dear Mr. Muddle," I began, I do not even have to pray about it. We were praying about it when the mail plane came with your letter asking us to consider returning to Prairie." Then I told him the whole story. "And praise the Lord for the assurance that my wife and baby are going to be all right," I added. "The Lord gave me that assurance as soon as I read your letter, because I could not expect you to take us on staff if Doloris were not well."

Doloris and Gordon flew home to Kentucky in January. I hired an Eskimo man to finish teaching her classes. The two older boys and I arrived in Louisville in May, four days before Alan was born. Although he arrived early like the rest of our children had been, he was healthy and chubby.

In July we returned to Prairie Bible Institute to begin my career as a Bible college teacher. Soon, I was doing everything I had wanted to do—teaching, radio announcing, preaching at a country church and going on spring ministry tours of churches in the U.S. and Canada. The Lord gave us a total of twenty-five years on Prairie staff.

I still haven't figured out what makes Doloris' faith so special, but God doesn't seem bothered much about whether I have or not.

93

God's Nudging

Alberta

Lesette, a student at Prairie Bible College, had come to my office for counseling on one or two occasions—no big problems, only requests for advice or guidance about studies. Often when young women sought counsel on personal matters, I referred them to my wife, but Lesette had never met Doloris.

On a Saturday evening, while grading papers at home, I felt burdened to pray for Lesette. The papers I was grading did not include hers; she was not taking that course, and I was not sure why I should have become concerned about her. After a moment of prayer, I returned to my grading, but the urge became much stronger. I had been asking the Lord to make me more sensitive to the guidance of the Holy Spirit in prayer, so I certainly did not want to ignore the insistent inner nudging.

After a few minutes, the conviction grew that Lesette needed help. I called to Doloris in the kitchen, "Honey, will you do something for me?"

"What do you want me to do?" she asked.

"It is difficult to explain," I said, "but there is a Bible

school student that I have been praying for, and I feel that she needs help. Will you go to see her?"

"Where does she live?"

"I don't know—one of the dorms. The switchboard is closed now, so you will have to inquire." (At that time, there were several dormitories for ladies.)

"What do you want me to say to her? What is her problem?" She obviously felt that I wasn't giving her much information and perhaps that the request was unreasonable.

"Honey, I know it may sound foolish, but I honestly don't know. I just feel that she needs help, and I can't very well go to a women's dorm on a Saturday night to see her. I would like for you to go. I don't know what you should say, but I think the Holy Spirit will direct you."

Doloris shook her head and mumbled, "Well, okay, if that is what you want."

The second door in the first dormitory she came to had Lesette's name above it. Doloris knocked. There was no answer. The room appeared to be dark. Doloris turned to go, but decided to knock again. She heard a chair scrape slightly on the floor and a voice called softly, "Come in."

"Oh, are you Mrs. Pike?" Lesette sobbed.

"Yes. I am. Why do you ask?"

Lesette sobbed again and said, " I was just sitting here by the window looking out at the stars and trying to sort things out in my mind. My mother is going blind, and I pray for her, but God doesn't answer. I wondered whether there really is a God or not, and if there is whether He ever pays any attention to me. Other people are always talking about God answering prayer, but it seems like He never answers my prayers. I looked into the sky and cried, 'God, if You are real, please send Mrs. Pike to help me.' That's when you knocked. I couldn't even answer for a minute."

94

Communing With God

Canada and India

Two of my students, Raja and Moni, came to my desk after class smiling with genuine joy, "My, you fellows look mighty happy today," I ventured. "Did you get a good letter from home?"

"No," replied Moni. "Well, that is not why we are so happy."

"Let me in on it. I'd like to rejoice with you. What gives you such joy?"

"This is the first time we ever knew that prayer is communion with God."

"Really?" We had just completed another class called Principles of Effective Prayer. Throughout the class, I taught that prayer is asking and receiving, confession, petition and intercession, thanksgiving and praise, warfare against Satan, and God's means of accomplishing His will on earth. I had pointed out that prayer is the most wonderful privilege, sacred duty, precious right, simple activity, powerful weapon and mysterious blessing that God has given to His children. But that day I had especially emphasized that prayer is communion with our Father.

"That's right," I continued, "you fellows have not known the Lord very long. I guess you could say that you are still babes in Christ. Tell me whether I am right—you were raised with a Hindu background, were led to the Lord while working in Saudi Arabia and soon after that came to Canada to study at Prairie Bible Institute. Do I have the events correct?"

"Yes, that's right," stated Raja, Moni's older brother. "But we never knew until today that prayer is communion with God! You said that in prayer we can have closer fellowship with God than the fellowship of brothers!"

"Yes."

"Or even the fellowship of a mother and child?"

"Yes, it is possible and more enduring."

"You said that our fellowship with God is closer even than the fellowship of a husband and wife." (Raja and Emily came to Canada already married. Moni married his wife Gloria after he graduated and returned to India.) I confirmed that I had made that very statement.

"That is why we are so happy. That is the best news we have ever heard," they declared.

I'll admit that I was quite surprised. Didn't all Christians know that? I had taken it for granted for so long that I assumed it was common knowledge.

"Tell me," I inquired, "what is the Hindu concept of prayer?"

Moni replied again, "If you need or want something, you go to the temple and give the priest a gift so he will intercede for you."

"Oh, so the idea of intercession was not entirely new when we studied that. But tell me, what kind of gift did you give to the priest?"

"That all depends on what you are asking him to pray for.

If it is a small thing, you give him a small gift; if it is a very big and important matter, you give a large gift."

"All right, let me suggest an example. Suppose the father in a family has been sick for six months. He has no income, the children are all hungry and there is no food in the house. What kind of gift would you give the priest to intercede for you?" I asked. (The reader needs to understand that in India there is no workmen's compensation, no welfare system, and no government-sponsored program of any kind to help a family in such a situation.)

"Oh," Moni answered in a tone of awe as Raja shook his head, "in that case we would probably give him a cow!"

"Really? I knew that cows were considered sacred in India, but I didn't know that you would give one to a priest to intercede for you."

"Yes, in such a terrible situation as that, we would probably give him a cow!" (A cow was apparently the most prized thing that came to their minds.) "But we never knew that *we* can actually have personal fellowship with God in prayer!"

Then the thought flashed across my mind that Hindus aren't the only ones with a very limited idea of prayer. I learned something from Raja and Moni that day. I went home and asked God never to let me take for granted again the communion I may have with Him through prayer. But I am a slow learner. I have to come back often and ask Him to teach me again and again.

At the time of this writing, Raja is a Superintendent over one hundred churches, two children's homes and two Christian schools in India. He is also Director of a Bible school recently started. He serves with SIM International. Moni, with Global Outreach, is pastor of a church that consists of former high-caste Hindus whom he has led to Christ. When we held prayer seminars for them in India, Moni's church was growing rapidly with newly baptized believers and has continued to grow since.

95

Somebody to Listen to!

Amsterdam

The Sabena Airlines waiting room in New York City was virtually deserted. Outside torrential rain obscured the view from the big window. I had four hours to wait. Great! What a time for reading and prayer!

"Lord, from Calgary to Toronto and from Toronto to New York, I have not been able to engage one person in a friendly conversation and have not had a good opportunity to witness to anyone. On the first flight the man beside me slept the whole trip. On the second one, I had the window on my right. The man on my left could hardly speak English, and the lady on the other side of him was engrossed in her paperback novel. Lord, on the flight to Amsterdam tonight, please give me someone to listen to."

Whoa! What did I say? "Someone to *listen* to?" Now, why did I say that? I had never prayed that before.

"Lord, . . . " I was going to modify my prayer a bit, but I stopped and thought, "No, that's okay, Lord. Let's just leave it as it is. If you put a talker beside me on this transatlantic flight and I listen, then he or she will be obliged to listen to me. It's a long flight."

On the 747, I sat in the left section, next to the window with two seats to my right. No one claimed the middle seat. Before the seat-belt light went on, the man on the aisle seat started talking. And I listened.

He was en route from Texas to Africa. He was in the precious-gem business. He had a house in Texas, a villa in Switzerland and a hotel suite in Liberia. He had written a book about his philosophy of life that he promised to send me but never did.

The gentleman was Jewish. A large group of a certain sect of Jews was aboard, and my friend explained a lot to me about their traditions. It so happened that he was raised in that particular sect, but he told me that he now considered them to be inconsistent and hypocritical. He admitted to being bitter because his father had forbidden him to marry a Gentile girl he had been in love with when he was a young man. But he soon launched into his philosophy.

All I had to do was show interest, listen and make small comments. In my thoughts I was saying, "Lord, You sure answered *that* one. I think You set me up for this. Or maybe You are setting him up. We'll see."

I finally got my chance. My Jewish friend had mentioned religion in general and certain religions in his discourse on philosophy. So I said, "As a Christian, I have a keen interest in hearing your observations about Christianity. I have met Jews who equated Adolf Hitler's atrocities with Christianity. Although you suffered through a German concentration camp, this is obviously not your viewpoint. I am very interested in learning what you, a modern Jew and student of philosophy, think constitutes a true Christian."

For the first time since boarding, he was quiet. He appeared to be deep in thought. At last he said, "Whether

Christian or Jew, Muslim or Hindu or whatever religion is of no consequence. I would say," he mused aloud, "that the important thing is that a person who is sincere in his efforts to please God by his good deeds."

Of course, that is what he had been pontificating for a couple of hours or more. I had been quite sure I knew before he did what he would say. Works and righteousness from start to finish, nothing more.

"Sir," I replied, "I appreciate your willingness to share your thoughts with me, a stranger. I believe that you have spoken from the sincerity of your heart. Would you care to hear my philosophy of life?"

"Oh . . . why, yes . . . of course. Your philosophy. Yes, of course."

"Well, to begin with, it is not really my philosophy. It was given to me by Someone else. But, yes, it is mine because I accepted it, and that makes it my own. It is based entirely on your Hebrew Scriptures and their fulfillment in the New Testament. One of your Hebrew scholars stated it succinctly. I have detected, in your openness to various ideas, a willingness to consider other ideas without being offended. Am I correct?"

He looked a bit confused, but answered, "Oh, yes, by all means, go right ahead."

"And you won't be offended," I insisted, "even if I show you that the teaching of the Bible is at odds with your philosophy, and, in fact, diametrically opposed to it?"

At this, he looked genuinely shocked. How could anyone possibly disagree with the position of toleration and good deeds that he had propounded? But he said, "Oh, no. No, that's fine. By all means tell me about this philosophy."

I pulled my New Testament from my jacket pocket and turned to Ephesians 2:8-9. I handed it to him to read: "For by grace are ye saved through faith; and that not of yourselves: it is the gift of God: Not of works, lest any man should boast" (KJV). He returned the New Testament to me, and I found Titus 3:5 and we read, "Not by works of righteousness which we have done, but according to his mercy he saved us, by the washing of regeneration, and renewing of the Holy Ghost." With a few questions and comments, I made sure he understood the importance of the verses. Then, I returned to Ephesians 2:10, "For we are his workmanship, created in Christ Jesus unto good works, which God has before ordained that we should walk in them."

"So you see," I declared, "good works are important, but they cannot save us. They cannot give us eternal life, because, 'All have sinned and come short of the glory of God,' as another New Testament verse tells us." Then I showed him Romans 3:23. "None of us could ever achieve God's standard by our own works. The only way to have His forgiveness and eternal life is to accept it as a free gift. Good works are the result, not the cause or origin of salvation." We looked at John 3:16 and John 1:12. His interest had become so genuine and intense that I talked to him about the Passover (Exodus 12), the Old Testament sacrifices and their New Testament fulfillment in Jesus Christ.

The hour was late and the plane's cabin lights were turned down.

The next morning, my Jewish friend graciously accepted my leather-bound New Testament as a gift. I wrote his name in it and wrote my address under my name. I made the analogy between his receiving that gift and God's offer of His Son as a free gift. He promised to read the New Testament. I hope he did.

I wrote to him and have prayed for him many times, but I have never heard from him. Will you pray for him now? God knows his name and whether he is still living. I will probably never see him again on this earth, but I hope to see him in heaven.

That day I learned an important principle about witnessing and praying: Listen.

96

A Prison With Grass

East Germany

While I was in Belgium as a Bible teacher with Operation Mobilization (OM) teams in the summer of 1980, Henk Wolthaus, an OM career missionary, invited me to go with him to East Germany, behind the Iron Curtain. That was nearly nine years before the collapse of Soviet communism, so missionaries were not permitted and OM had no work in East Germany. Nevertheless Henk, who was from the Netherlands, went into East Germany periodically as a tourist. While there, he found believers and churches to encourage and help. Of course, I jumped at the chance to go.

I crossed West Germany by train and met Henk in Nurnberg. In his little European Ford we drove to East Germany. I was surprised at how easily we crossed the border. We filled out a few identification papers and paid a fee. I made sure I had only my Canadian Passport and other Canadian identification with me because Henk assured me that it would be less difficult than entering as an American. (I have dual citizenship.) However, I was keenly aware of the plowed mine strip that stretched as far as I could see on either side of the road at the border. Seeing the towers with gun turrets spaced along that strip made cold chills run down my back as I remembered stories I had read about the East Germans who tried to escape their homeland.

In Plauen (pronounced "plowen") we went to the police station and registered as required. Henk did the talking because I don't speak German. The man at the desk kept looking at me and questioning Henk. Later Henk told me the man felt sure he had seen me before, but Henk assured him that I was a tourist from Canada and had never been in Germany before. He finally gave us the proper permits.

We sauntered about the city, observing the great open spaces that remained from Allied bombings in World War II. I bought some lace doilies for my wife and ate a meal at a department-store café. I had never seen such a bland, gray city. The men's room in the department store was filthy beyond description. The food in the large café, served through a little window, offered only two choices of meals. I ordered meal number one by holding up one finger and Henk ordered the other. Both were tasteless. But the people were all very warm and friendly.

Finally, we began looking for the campground that Henk knew was somewhere near. Anytime we stopped to look at a map, a kind German person would immediately come over to offer directions. (Henk's foreign Ford was very obvious, not only because of the license plates, but also because all the other cars were little Russian Ladas and all looked alike. Apparently there had been no change in models or styles in years.)

When we inquired about directions to the camp, the gentleman who had stopped to help said, "Just follow me," (in German, of course). He led us about four miles out of town to the camp. However, by that time it was raining steadily and the ground was muddy, so we decided to sleep in the car instead of putting up our tent. It was cramped, but we were tired and we slept.

About 2 o'clock in the morning, we were awakened by a powerful light shining in our eyes. There were policemen on each side of the car shining very strong lights into the car. They gruffly demanded to know who we were and what we were doing. Henk showed them our permits and the camping equipment in the trunk. They did not seem convinced, but after a few minutes let us go back to sleep.

The next day we drove around the countryside until dusk, when we arrived in the small town of Marknewkirchen ("Mark's New Church") near the Czechoslovakian border.

The pastor was waiting at his home for us. Henk had been there before and carried addresses and directions in his head. As soon as we arrived, the pastor took us to the church. It was not an underground, unregistered church. It was registered with the communist government but was not allowed a sign or identification of any kind in front. It looked like any drab warehouse. After passing through a windowless room and groping for the one pull-string light, we went into the sanctuary. The walls were painted white and there were windows on one side; the pews were plain board benches. (The big Lutheran state church about two blocks away was a fine cathedral, and it was the only one allowed to show any identity as a church.)

For six days, for three hours in the morning and three hours in the afternoon, I taught a group of about twenty university-age people about prayer. Of course, about half that time was taken up by the woman who had come from East Berlin to translate for me. After two days, I learned that the young people spoke fairly good English—more grammatically correct than many in North America. They had studied Russian from grade one and English from grade seven throughout their school careers. They were too shy to let me know they spoke English until they became better acquainted with me. Each evening the families came for a three-hour service (including translation and prayer time). The students in the youth group came from several towns, and I was pleased that such a large crowd had come to hear me. Then I learned that they came to the church for a prayer meeting every evening after supper. They were there for the Lord, not for me!

A good percentage of each meeting was devoted to prayer. I soon realized I was probably learning more than I was teaching. The young folks prayed for their friends who were out in the campgrounds witnessing for Christ. About half of the group took half of their two-week vacation from work to attend the prayer seminar while the other half camped and witnessed to people with whom they played shuffleboard, horseshoes or badminton. The following week, the half that had studied with me would share pup tents at night with the others and teach them what they had learned in the seminar.

The pastor's prayers shook my Western presuppositions. In spite of the fact that he knew there were always one or two communist informers in the congregation, he prayed prayers like this one: "Oh, my God, we have sinned. Now our land is divided, and we are under the heel of the oppressor. Father, we are in a prison with grass. We are in bondage to our enemies, the atheists. But, God, we confess that we sinned against You, and You are righteous in all that You have allowed to come upon Germany, because we dared to lift our fists against Your people, the Jews. But Lord, we are Your people. We have been bought with the blood of Your Son, our Lord Jesus Christ. And You said, 'If my people, who are called by my name, will humble themselves and pray and seek my face and turn from their wicked ways, then will I hear from heaven and will forgive their sin and will heal their land' (2 Chronicles 7:14). Lord, we are Your people called by Your name; we call ourselves *Christians* because we follow Christ. But our land is divided. Hear our prayer and heal our land, dear Father."

"A prison with grass?" The plowed mine strips and gun turrets separating East Germany from the free world were fresh in my mind, and I understood. But as I prayed with the pastor, who was about my age, I realized that, had we been a year older, we might have fought each other in World War II. And I wept as I heard his humble, honest confession to God for his people. He had not said, "Our fathers sinned," or "Adolf Hitler is the guilty one," but, "Father, we have sinned." He confessed, "We dared to lift our fists against Your people the Jews."

During that trip I learned to pray, "Father, teach me to identify with the needs of sinners—my people." My German brother was not old enough to be personally responsible for the Nazi atrocities. Nor was Daniel old enough to have been personally responsible for the sins of his people that led to their captivity. Yet Daniel prayed, "We have sinned and done wrong. We have been wicked and have rebelled; we have turned away from your commands and laws" (Daniel 9:5).

When I asked the young people whether any would escape to the West if it were possible, they expressed genuine amazement at the thought.

"No, of course not! Who would tell our people about

Jesus? You from the West cannot come as missionaries. We are the only ones to tell them."

I remembered my prayers for the Soviet bloc countries when I had stood on the shores of the Bering Strait and had looked across at the Siberian mountains. And I still pray for them. But since I prayed with the East German pastor and his flock, my brothers and sisters in Christ, there is a difference in my prayers.

97

Prayer for a Tyrant

Uganda

Doloris and I listened to the ten o'clock news from CBC (Canadian Broadcasting Corporation). The newscaster reported about the genocide in Uganda under the military dictator Idi Amin. Amin's army was slaughtering thousands of Ugandans in a "Christian" tribe.

After the newscast, we had our prayer time together. I couldn't get Amin off my mind. I almost prayed, "Lord, kill him!" But I realized that, not only would it not be a very nice prayer, but also God had predetermined the tyrant's lifespan before he was born. Instead, I prayed, "Lord, I am like Paul was when he wrote Romans 8:26-27. I don't know what I ought to pray. Please teach me how to pray in accordance with your will concerning this man and this situation."

I knew that Idi Amin knew the gospel and had knowingly rejected Christ. I had read about it in Prairie Bible Institute's library in a book by a missionary to Uganda who had personally shared the plan of salvation with Amin. He knew other missionaries who had done so also. Idi Amin had several wives and many children. His children had been educated in schools operated by Christian missions. But the missionary author said that Amin had a deep-seated hatred of God and Jesus Christ.

As I prayed, I said, "Lord, your honor is at stake. This ruthless dictator is not only guilty of genocide; he is challenging Your authority. He is from a Muslim tribe and is deliberately attacking a Christian tribe. Lord, rebuke the devil, I pray. And I resist the devil in the name of Jesus Christ my Lord and Savior, who has 'all authority in heaven and on earth' (Matthew 28:18). Lord, remove Idi Amin from his throne." It was not my task to determine how he was to be removed, but I had no doubt that it was God's will that I ask Him to remove the God-hating leader before he could kill more Christians.

When we concluded our prayer time, the thought entered my mind, "Who do you think you are? Two little nobodies on the western prairies of Canada—you don't really think that you can influence the affairs of a mighty dictator and his vicious army on the other side of the world with your little prayer, do you?"

"Get behind me, Satan. You are defeated by the blood of Jesus Christ," I insisted, "and in His name I reject your suggestions." I knew we didn't have any power in ourselves, and I would not dare try to stand against the devil in any merit other than that of Jesus Christ. But we are not told to flee from the devil. We are told, "Flee the evil desires of youth" (2 Timothy 2:22), and "Submit…to God. Resist the devil, and he will flee from you" (James 5:7). Doubtful thoughts did not bother me any more.

The next night I prayed the same thing.

After the third or fourth night, the CBC Newscaster said that the Ugandan tyrant, Idi Amin, had been driven from his throne and was fleeing the country.

A few years later, Doloris and I attended a Change-the-World School of Prayer seminar in Calgary. The seminar leader said, "A few years ago there was a godless dictator in Uganda named Idi Amin." Suddenly, he had riveted my attention. He told almost identically the details of the story I have just related to you—how he and his wife, praying together, had felt led to pray for God to remove Amin from power and God had done so just a few days later. Then, he added, "and in almost every major city where I tell this story, someone comes up afterward and says, 'That's amazing! That is exactly what happened to me and my wife (or my husband).'"

The seminar leader commented that it seemed that it was always husband-and-wife teams praying together that had sensed God leading them to pray the same prayer at approximately the same time. Of course, there could have been many others that I won't hear about until we get Home to Glory, but I know that God does bless husband-and-wife prayer teams. Oh, how I thank God for a wife who has always prayed with me.

It seems that God has a lot of "little nobodies" spread across prairies, farmlands, mountains and valleys, in many cities and towns, villages and country places. Jesus said, "Again, I tell you that if two of you on earth agree about anything you ask for, it will be done for you by my Father in heaven. For where two or three come together in my name, there am I with them" (Matthew 18:19-20). He did not say "two kings," "two presidents or prime-ministers," "two ambassadors," not even "two great prayer warriors." He just said, "two of you on earth." No matter where I look in Scripture I find that VIP's don't have any priority for God's attention! James 1:5 actually says, "If any of you lacks wisdom, he should ask God." That's why so often, I say, "Thank You, Lord. Count me in; I'm fully qualified!"

98

As for God, His Ways Are Perfect

Alberta

"Please pray for my husband Len," pleaded Joan Brouwer.

"Yes," added the pastor of the church in Provost, Alberta. "Len has had a cough for a couple of weeks and can't seem to shake it off. Let's remember him in prayer."

"Pastor, I don't quite know how to explain this," Joan added. "Although Len is ill, I am more concerned right now about his attitude and spiritual welfare. Like you say, he has had this bad cough for a while and can't get rid of it.

"He was anointed and prayed for by the elders of the church according to James 5:14 last week, and he has been sure that the Lord would miraculously heal him. In fact, he set a deadline and prayed specifically that the healing would come by today. He promised God that he would come to church today and testify to everyone about the Lord's healing him."

Joan continued with her story, "At ten o'clock last night he said, 'The Lord still has two hours to do it.' Then, he played the piano and sang, 'Bring Your Vessels, Not a Few.' Well, midnight came, but no healing. He was sure God was going to heal him. Hadn't he followed biblical principle? He thought he would be back in church today with a glowing testimony for the Lord, but instead he is at home and very despondent. He doesn't know what to make of it. It looks to him as though God has let him down. Please pray about his attitude, his despondency."

I was the visiting speaker at the church that Sunday and heard Joan's impassioned plea for prayer. My heart went out to her and Len in sympathy.

I had heard about Len Brouwer, a man whose Christian testimony was widely known, but I had not met him. I knew about his great burden for missions and hoped that he might become a prayer-partner with us as we returned to Alaska the very next day. I struggled as I tried to find words to pray for Joan's request. My wife and I had been through something similar when our son was healed instantaneously of hepatitis, but the Lord had not healed Doloris and me in the same way.

In the churchyard after the evening service, Alf Aizzier said, "I don't like the looks of your trailer hitch. I have a welding outfit on the farm and can put on a better one for you."

The job took all day, Monday. My mind was not so much on the trailer problems as on Len Brouwer. As we had supper with the pastor Monday evening, I asked, "Where do the Brouwers live? I would like to meet Len."

"Yes, I wish you would," he replied, and he gave me directions to Len's bakery. "The Brouwers live in the apartment above the bakery."

Joan and her daughters showed me through the bakery, including Len's Gospel Book corner, set apart for the display and sale of Bibles and Christian books. Then, we went upstairs.

Len was a very thin man with a wracking cough, but he welcomed me warmly. He was obviously a radiant Christian, but there was a look of anxiety in his eyes.

"Len, I have heard about you and your zeal for Christ," I commented, "and I have looked forward to meeting you. I am sorry you couldn't be at the services yesterday. Perhaps the Lord kept me here an extra day so we could get acquainted and visit."

I then told him the story of our son's healing and how God had worked differently when Doloris and I contracted the same disease. We discussed James 5 and Paul's thorn in the flesh in 2 Corinthians 12. We also talked about Jesus' intense prayer in the Garden of Gethsemane and His submission to the Father, "Yet not my will, but Yours be done" (Luke 22:42).

When it was time to leave, Len, Joan, their nearly grown children and I prayed Jesus' Gethsemane prayer for Len.

Some weeks later in Alaska, we received a letter from Joan: "Len has lung cancer. But he is happy in the Lord. Ever since the night you visited us he has had peace. There is no anxiety. He says that he wants his life to count for Christ whether by life or by death."

The second letter arrived a few months later: "Len is with the Lord. He had a wonderful victory through it all. Twice a week, he had to go to Edmonton, about 190 miles each way, for treatments. The people of Provost volunteered to drive for him, so I could take care of the bakery. Twice each week during that time, he has had a different driver, often an unsaved friend, to witness to all the way to Edmonton and back."

Since Len went Home, the Lord has opened many doors for Joan to speak to others about Christ and His strengthening and comforting power in time of trouble. She declares, "As for God, His way is perfect" (2 Samuel 22:31).

[illegible] years [illegible] road [illegible] but no [illegible] obvious [illegible] Christian [illegible] was a loss [illegible] in his eyes.

[illegible] have [illegible] and your zeal for Christ [illegible] and I have [illegible] your [illegible] yesterday [illegible] so [illegible]

[illegible] told [illegible] God [illegible] when Donna and I [illegible] Paul [illegible] 2 Corinthians [illegible] We also talked about [illegible] and [illegible] and His [illegible]

[illegible] to [illegible] God [illegible] and I [illegible] prayed [illegible] There is no [illegible] for Christ [illegible]

The second letter arrived a few [illegible] Lewis [illegible] a wonderful [illegible] had [illegible] 180 [illegible] to [illegible] one of [illegible] each week [illegible] drive [illegible] the way [illegible] and back.

[illegible] the Lord has another [illegible] for [illegible] and [illegible] in time of trouble [illegible]

99

The God of Thieves

India

"How many gods do the Hindus have?" I asked Raja, a former student from Prairie Bible Institute.

"Nobody knows," he replied. "Thousands. They have a god for everything. When you don't have a god for something, you create another one."

"Man creating god in his own image?"

"Something like that."

We were standing at the pharmacy counter facing the sidewalk while the proprietor went back to a shelf to get me some cough drops. I looked up at a large poster on the pharmacy wall next to me. It was the picture of one of the Hindu gods.

"That's the god of thieves," commented Raja.

"Huh?" I was shocked. "What did you say?"

"That's the god of thieves," he repeated.

"That's what I thought you said," I answered stupidly. "You are pulling my leg."

"No I'm not. After all, everyone has to have a god to make them successful in their work. That's the god thieves pray to—to make them successful in picking your pocket."

I paid for the cough drops and counted my change very carefully.

100

Lost Boy

India

I had had a fever and sore throat all day. I had lost my voice and could not go to teach the prayer seminar that night. I hoarsely asked Raja to teach it. He had taken my class, Principles of Effective Prayer, in Canada some years before and had translated for me almost every night in various south Indian villages in recent weeks. I was sure he could teach it as well without me. Doloris went with Raja and his wife Emily to the new village.

When Doloris came in about midnight, I was still awake, so she related the events of the evening. Yes, of course, Raja had taught well. At least she assumed he had, since she could not understand the Tamil language.

"But," she said, "the people were very disappointed that you were not able to go. They prayed for you, that you would be well enough tomorrow night to go, even if all you can do is sit with them or just give a short testimony."

She also told me that at about nine o'clock, just as everyone was ready to leave, a woman had come into the little church crying. She said that her son had not come home from school that afternoon when the other village children arrived. She waited hour after hour. Although she had wanted to come to the seminar, the twelve-year-old boy still had not come home. She was beside herself with worry. At nearly nine o'clock, she decided to come to the church to ask for prayer for her son's safe return.

The next morning I awoke feeling fine. No fever and no sore throat. I wasn't even hoarse!

That evening when we drove into the village, where I had not yet been, the people were out in force to welcome us. Elderly men and women, mothers with babies, boys blowing battered trumpets, and girls dancing around with tambourines—it seemed the whole village had turned out. As we proceeded slowly, we began to understand what they were chanting: "God answered *both* of our prayers!" Then, we realized the celebration was not only that I was well and able to come, but the boy must have been safely at home as well.

On the way home from school, the boy had stopped to get a drink from a pipe where water was running. When he turned to pick up his schoolbooks from the rock where he had laid them moments before, they were gone. Someone had stolen them the moment his back was turned!

What was he to do? He knew his family had no money to buy more books. Fearing he would be punished, he was afraid to go home, so he began walking.

At nine o'clock that night, a Hindu lady in a distant town felt compelled to go out to her front yard. Yet, she was afraid—of the dark, of robbers and of evil spirits. She never opened her door after dark. But she felt she must go. She did not know why, but she knew she must.

Opening the front door, she heard a child whimper. Against all her traditional instincts and fears, she went to the bushes and found the runaway boy. Taking him into her house, she learned his name, his village and why he was so far from home at night.

Meanwhile, the mother's fears had become unbearable and she had gone to the church. At that moment the whole congregation, with the pastor, the superintendent and his wife and Doloris, all prayed for the boy's safe return. They knew that the mother's extreme fears were based on a harsh reality.

Children are often kidnapped in India. The kidnappers cut off one of the child's hands or a foot so he or she will be more effective in begging from tourists in Bombay, Delhi, Calcutta or some other large city. The kidnappers give the children just enough food to keep them alive but very thin and emaciated. Their owners make their money this way. We had wondered why there were so many beggars (children as well as adult or even elderly people) who had only one hand or foot. One old man, who had perhaps been kidnapped as a child, hobbled on a homemade crutch down the aisle of the train we had traveled on to Madras.

The lost boy's mother was sure her son had been kidnapped. By the time he had been gone for nearly six hours, the kidnappers would have cut off his hand or foot.

The Hindu woman, who had feared the dark, took the boy home on a bus. The people in his village could hardly believe that he had walked so far in six hours.

There was much rejoicing in the village the next evening when they saw me in the car with Raja, Emily and Doloris. "God has answered both of our prayers!" the believers sang out loudly enough for all the Hindus to hear as they ran and danced along on both sides of the little dirt road leading to the church.

Both the boy and his mother wanted him to be dedicated to God for the ministry. After I taught the seminar with Raja's help, we questioned the mother and son about it, prayed a prayer of thanksgiving and asked for spiritual discernment. Then we dedicated the happy boy to the Lord for His glory.

"Raja," I asked while he was visiting in our home in Canada eight years later, "what ever happened to the little boy who . . .?"

Before I could finish, Raja answered, "Oh, he is going on with the Lord and planning to go to Bible school to study for the ministry."

101

God Sent You[23]

India

After a half-hour drive from Joshua's house to the train station in Lucknow (a city in Utter Pradesh, India), we arrived at five in the morning and were greeted by a large chalkboard announcing that our train was rescheduled for ten o'clock that morning. The tracks had been bombed.

Temples and mosques had been destroyed. One of our seminars had been canceled because the city was under a military ban. (Essentially this meant that there could be no meetings, no visitors from outside and residents were restricted to their homes after two in the afternoon.) Other than this, we had not been affected by the war between Hindus and Muslims. Now the war was an actual reality, so we returned to Joshua's house.

Before leaving again at nine, Joshua and his wife Reena joined hands with Doloris and me in prayer. "Lord, give the Pikes someone to share the gospel with on the train today," he prayed.

At ten o'clock the train was ready. Joshua put our suitcases on the rack above our seat as I prayed silently, "Lord, please send some strong young man to help me get that luggage down tonight in New Delhi." (I had a "frozen rotator cuff." Although I didn't learn why or what it was called until we got back to a North American orthopedic surgeon, I could not lift my right arm.) Those extraordinarily high luggage racks were a major obstacle!

"Where are you folks from?" asked a voice in fluent English, as we waved to Joshua. Turning, we saw a strikingly handsome young Indian man whose face was almost between ours.

"We are from Canada," I replied.

"Oh, what brings you to our country? Are you tourists?"

"No, not exactly," I hesitated. "Well, yes, people have been very gracious in showing us many extraordinary sights, but we have been holding prayer seminars in Christian churches in south India for two months and in north India for one month."

"Really? I believe in prayer!" was his unexpected comment as he came around into the aisle to face us. "At least I think I do. Sometimes I'm not sure. One day I think God could do anything, but the next day, I am not sure there even is a God."

A little bell went off in my mind: "Someone to share the gospel with on the train today." Prayer request number one!

Before I could reply, Ashok changed the subject: "Where are you going now?" He was squatting down so we could be at the same eye level.

"To New Delhi."

"No, I mean what is your destination?"

"Oh, we have to get an airplane back to Canada."

"How will you get from the train station in New Delhi to the airport?"

"We'll have to get a taxi because it will be after nine

tonight when we get there. Our plane leaves at six tomorrow morning, and we have to be at the Air India counter three hours beforehand because of the tight security. I understand it is a long way from the train station to the air terminal; it would hardly be worthwhile to go to a hotel. We'll have to take a taxi and then sit up the rest of the night."

Will you let me do something for you?" asked Ashok. "When we get to New Delhi tonight, will you let me negotiate a taxi for you? When they see your white face, they'll take you all over Delhi and New Delhi and keep right on running that meter up. You can't do a thing about it, because you won't know where you are anyway. I can negotiate with a cab driver for you to prepay, and he will go right to the terminal. I know how far it is and about how much it should cost you."

"Great!" I said exuberantly. "Yes, I know about prepaying, and that will be a tremendous help. By the way, since you are so generous in helping a stranger, may I ask you for another favor? I hurt my shoulder and can't move my arm much, and...."

Ashok interrupted, "Oh, I'll get that luggage down for you when we get to New Delhi." Prayer request number two!

"Honey, why don't you go back and sit with Ashok so he won't have to stay there in the aisle to talk?" suggested Doloris. The seat beside him was empty. "I'll write some letters." I knew that was not all she would be doing!

Twenty-one-year-old Ashok, whose father was of one of India's wealthy class and a Brahman (the highest caste in the Hindu system), was a student at the University of Moscow in Russia. He spoke Hindi, Russian and English fluently and was starting a computer software company in Moscow.

There, he had fallen in love with a fellow Indian student from a family of a bit lower caste than his. He had been quite sure that his father would go through the roof when he heard that Ashok wanted to marry a girl of a lower caste, but to his amazement his father had been quite open-minded about it. In fact, his father and mother had gone to the girl's home city in the eastern part of India to meet with her parents and arrange the engagement and wedding. Ashok was on his way home from there when we met.

"The plane I had planned to take to New Delhi was hijacked on the way in yesterday," he explained. "They caught the hijacker but would not let the plane go until they checked it thoroughly. There is no telling how long that will take. My parents decided to wait for it, but I didn't want to wait, so I took the train instead."

I brought the subject back to prayer and then to Jesus Christ. When I opened my Bible and read from John 3 to him, he leaned over, eager to read every word. That afternoon, he bowed his head in prayer with me and received Jesus Christ into his heart.

I fell asleep. When I awoke, Ashok was waiting to talk more.

"Mr. Pike," he said, "that book that you read from, that was a Bible, wasn't it?"

"Why, yes, it was." It had not occurred to me that he might not know. I had referred to it as "God's Word."

"I never saw a Bible before," he stated in awe. "Well, I don't think I have. At least, I know that I had never read a word from a Bible," he continued in a hushed tone.

Later, he added, "It's strange that I should have spent the day talking to you. The couple on the other side of the aisle, the ones with the baby . . . I was talking to them when you got on the train. They are about my age and . . . how do you say it? I mean, you are older, and . . . what do they call it in English?"

"The generation gap?" I asked.

"Yes, 'generation gap,' that's it."

"But you see, Ashok, there is a very good reason why you chose to stay with me today. God sent you to me in answer to prayer. Remember, I told you how I prayed for a strong young man to help me with my luggage?"

"Yes!"

"And how my friend Joshua prayed that God would send someone we could share the gospel with on the train? That's what we have been doing, isn't it?"

"We sure have," he declared, in that hushed, awe-filled tone again. "But, Mr. Pike, God sent you in answer to my prayer!"

"Really?" I asked. "What had you prayed, Ashok?"

"Three days ago, I prayed for God to send an older man to teach me the true way!"

I gave Ashok my Bible and handwritten instructions to help him find the chapters and verses we had read together. I also gave him helps for starting daily Bible study. He took my luggage down for me, and his father's chauffeur, who met him with the family limousine, negotiated the taxi fare for us.

Philip had a similar experience (Acts 8:26-40). The Ethiopian Treasurer was seeking the true way. He had been to Jerusalem to worship the true God and was reading Isaiah 53:7-8, when an angel of the Lord directed Philip to him to share the gospel with him. He believed, was baptized and the Spirit took Philip away.

---

[23]The name *Ashok* is fictional; all other details are factual.

Other titles available from Gabriel Publishing...

Contact us for details on any of these books -
PO Box 1047, Waynesboro, GA 30830
Tel: (706) 554-1594   Fax: (706) 554-7444
Toll-Free: 1-8MORE-BOOKS
e-mail: gabriel@omlit.om.org

God's Great Ambition
Dan & Dave Davidson & George Verwer
ISBN: 1-884543-69-3

This unique collection of quotes and Scriptures has been designed to motivate thousands of people into action in world missions. George Verwer and the Davidsons are well-known for their ministries of mission mobilization as speakers and writers. Prepare to be blasted out of your comfort zone by this spiritual dynamite!

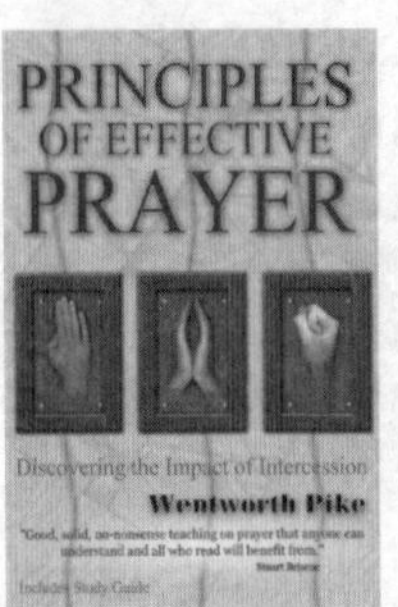

Principles of Effective Prayer
Wentworth Pike
ISBN: 1-884543-65-0

What is prayer? Why pray? Created as a devotional study for individuals or a textbook for groups, *Principles of Effective Prayer* answers these questions and many others. Developed as a class taught at Prairie Bible Institute (Canada), this book will lead you into a life and ministry of effective, God-glorifying prayer!

The Cross and The Crescent
Understanding the Muslim Heart and Mind
Phil Parshall
ISBN: 1-884543-68-5

Living as a missionary among Muslims, Phil Parshall understands the Muslim heart and mind. In this very personal book, he looks at what Muslims believe and how their beliefs affect - and don't affect - their behavior. He compares and contrasts Muslim and Christian views on the nature of God, sacred Scriptures, worship, sin and holiness, Jesus and Muhammed, human suffering, and the afterlife.

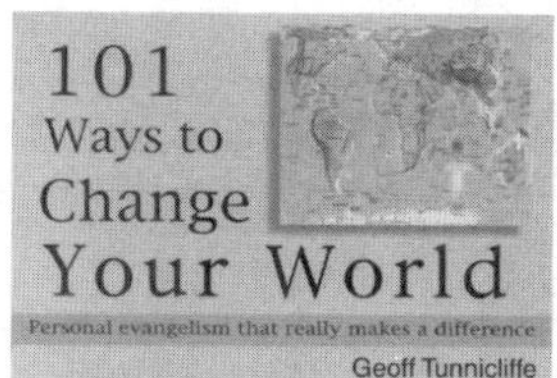

101 Ways to Change Your World
Geoff Tunnicliffe
ISBN: 1-884543-49-9

Geoff Tunnicliffe has compiled an invaluable collection of ways to change the world in his newly revised *101 Ways to Change Your World.* In addition to 101 practical ways to put faith into action, Tunnicliffe has also included statistics and resources for individuals desiring to make a difference in God's World.

Street Boy
Fletch Brown
ISBN: 1-884543-64-2

Jaime Jorka, a street boy in the Philippines, lays a challenge before the missionary whose wallet he has stolen - and discovers for himself what Jesus can do. This true-to-life story reveals the plight of street children worldwide and shows that they too can be won to Christ. "The lot of the street children of the world is a guilty secret that needs to be exposed and addressed. This book does it admirably." - Stuart Briscoe

Operation World
21st Century Edition
Patrick Johnstone & Jason Mandryk
ISBN: 1-85078-357-8

The definitive prayer handbook for the church is now available in its 21st Century Edition containing 80% new material! Packed with informative and inspiring fuel for prayer about every country in the world, *Operation World* is essential reading for anyone who wants to make a difference! Over 2,000,000 in print! Recipient of 2002 ECPA Gold Book Award.

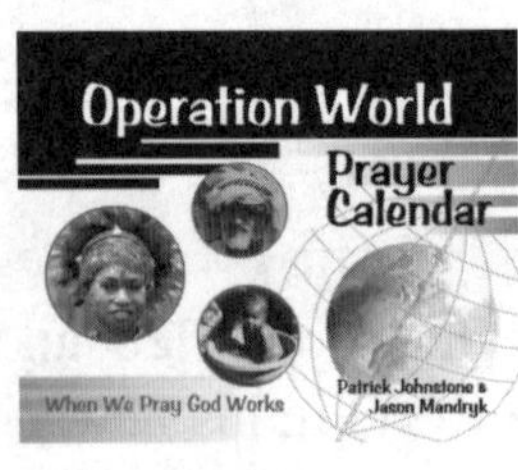

Operation World Prayer Calendar
ISBN: 1-884543-59-6

This spiral desk calendar contains clear graphics and useful geographic, cultural, economic, and political statistics on 122 countries of the world, the *Operation World Prayer Calendar* is a great tool to help you pray intelligently for the world. Pray for each country for three days and see how God works!

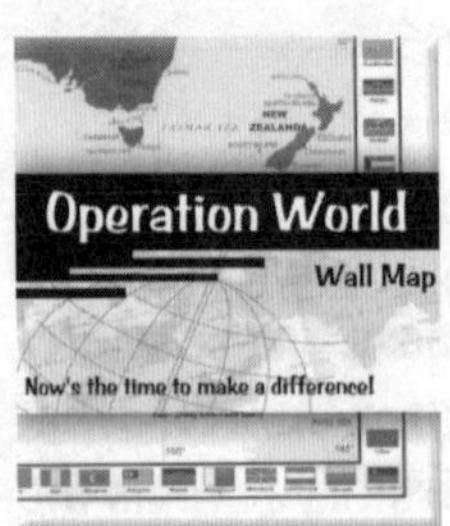

Operation World Wall Map
22" x 36"
ISBN: 1-884543-60-X (Laminated)
ISBN: 1-884543-61-8 (Folded)

This beautiful, full-color wall map is a great way to locate the countries each day that you are praying for and build a global picture. Not only an excellent resource for schools, churches, and offices, but a valuable tool for the home.

The Challenge of Missions
Oswald J. Smith
ISBN: 1-884543-02-2

Almost 2000 years have passed and the desire of Jesus that all should hear his good news is as strong as ever. In this remarkable book Oswald J. Smith maintains that the church which takes this command seriously will experience the blessing of God. *The Challenge of Missions*, which has sold more than 100,000 copies since its first publication, remains compelling reading in this period of exciting growth of the Church worldwide.

Dr. Thomas Hale's Tales of Nepal

Living Stones of the Himalayas
ISBN: 1-884543-35-9
Don't Let the Goats Eat the Loquat Trees
ISBN: 1-884543-36-7
On the Far Side of Liglig Mountain
ISBN: 1-884543-34-0

These fascinating accounts of the true-life stories of doctors Tom and Cynthia Hale share everyday and incredible experiences of life with the beguiling character and personalities of the Nepalese people. In sharing these experiences the reader is truly transported to a most enchanting land.